AT HOME WITH FRIENDS

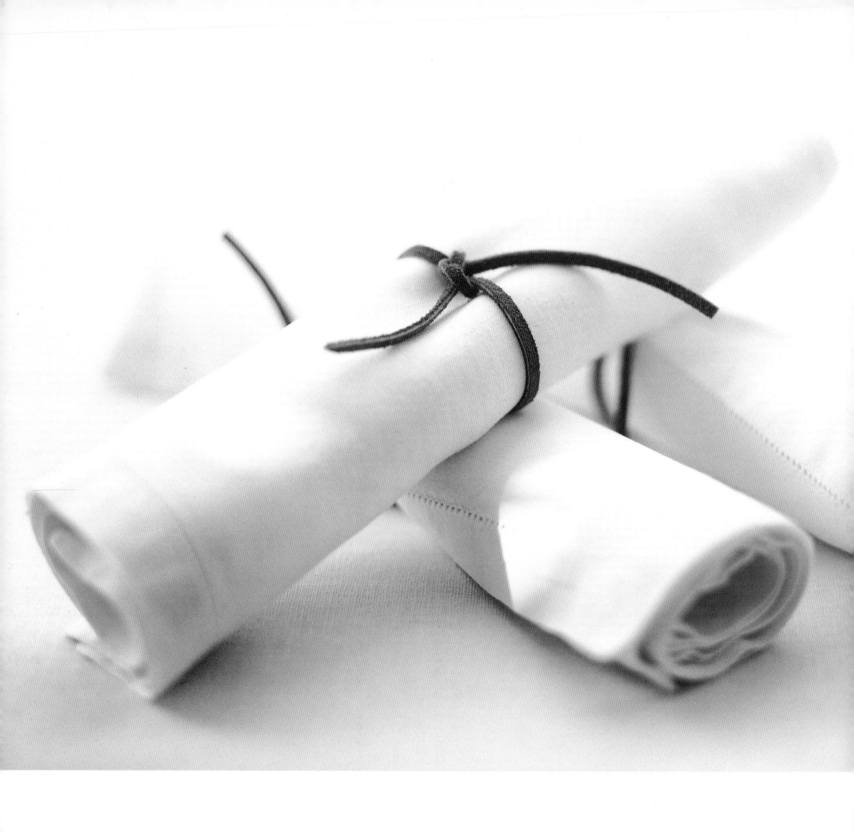

by michele adams and gia russo photographs by victoria pearson
recipes by kimberly huson

AT HOME WITH FRIENDS

SPONTANEOUS CELEBRATIONS FOR ANY OCCASION

CHRONICLE BOOKS
SAN FRANCISCO

Text copyright © 2002 by Michele Adams and Gia Russo.
Photographs copyright © 2002 by Victoria Pearson.
All rights reserved. No part of this book may be reproduced in any form
without written permission from the publisher.

Library of Congress Cataloging-in-Publication Data available.

ISBN: 0-8118-3344-5

Manufactured in China

Designed by Design: MW

Recipe development and food styling by Kimberly Huson
and Ronnda Hamilton

Distributed in Canada by Raincoast Books
9050 Shaughnessy Street
Vancouver, British Columbia V6P 6E5

10 9 8 7 6 5 4 3 2 1

Chronicle Books LLC
85 Second Street
San Francisco, California 94105

www.chroniclebooks.com

DEDICATION

To my mom, for inspiring and encouraging me more than she could imagine. Her gracious style of entertaining and her generous spirit have filled my life with so much happiness. And to my husband, John, who is always up for a great party.

—MICHELE

For my wonderful husband, Michael, who supports and encourages me, and for my parents, who showed me nothing is impossible. —GIA

ACKNOWLEDGMENTS

There are many people whose wisdom, kindness, talent, and generosity made *At Home with Friends* possible. We would like to acknowledge and thank them for helping us to fulfill another dream. Without their selfless efforts and cooperation, none of this would be possible.

We would like to thank Mikyla Bruder, our editor, for standing by our sides and guiding us through another rewarding experience. Our gratitude and admiration also goes to photographer Victoria Pearson, who captured our ideas with sheer brilliance and brought light and energy to the entire project, and her assistant John Nakano. Kimberly Huson and Ronnda Hamilton, our incredible food stylists, worked their magic both on set and afterwards, developing the wonderful recipes that fill our menus.

Many thanks to the following friends and family who graciously allowed us to shoot in their beautiful homes: Jacqueline and John Adams, Lorie Gianulli, and Kimberly and Don Corsini. We would also like to thank Kamal Sandhu of Shelter, Mary Ellen Monahan of Soolip Bungalow, and Denise Riglau of Calvin Klein for loaning us furniture and accessories from our favorite stores.

With the pace of life accelerating each and every day, we often lose touch with the things that give our lives meaning. One of those things is time spent in the company of family and friends. Many of us cherish memories of loved ones gathered together for warm summer night barbecues or festive holiday cocktail parties, and many recall a time when company gathered on Sundays for a hearty meal and lively conversation. Although we remember those occasions fondly, most of us find it impossible to maintain such traditions today. Just finding time to sit down to a dinner with our immediate families is challenging enough, let alone gathering a group of friends and relatives. But it's those very gatherings, those singular moments, that make our lives special and make all of our long, hard workdays worthwhile.

When we decided to create *At Home with Friends*, our goal was to produce a book of simple ideas and recipes that would enable a time-pressed generation to rediscover the time-honored traditions of entertaining. We wanted to create parties that could be planned on a realistic schedule and modest budget, with all the style and flair of modern living. We wanted to encourage people to get together with spontaneity, and to offer ideas for truly easy, last-minute party preparation. We wanted to create recipes that required minimal ingredients, with easy-to-follow instructions, and to include plenty of store-bought options in case there isn't time to cook. We wanted to provide inexpensive, low-effort decorating ideas that can be accomplished without the help of a glue gun. Finally, we wanted to create a book that inspires readers to get their families and friends together to enjoy the simple pleasure of entertaining. Sure, most of us won't be able to add a weekly dinner party to our sixty-hour workweeks, but we can at least squeeze a cocktail party or a barbecue in here or there.

In the pages that follow we present ten unique parties divided into five categories: breakfasts, outdoor entertaining, dinner parties, buffets, and cocktail parties. Each chapter is organized in a simple and easy-to-follow format. Each chapter covers a particular kind of party, with specific, practical information about hosting that party—from how to best set up a buffet to the ins and outs of planning a successful cocktail party. Within the chapters, you'll find menus and timelines for parties with a variety of different moods and styles, enough to suit any occasion. In Chapter Five, for example, we present both a classic holiday cocktail party as well as a slightly more unusual party featuring drinks and hors d'oeuvres that take their cues from India—two very different parties in design and menu, both very easy to plan and host.

At the heart of modern entertaining is one basic idea: Make your guests feel at home. To that end, we present simple and delicious menus and recipes, ideas and tips for creating mood and ambience with a few simple touches, and timesavers and store-bought foods to facilitate easy planning and preparation (because a relaxed host is a good host). Whether you have a few hours or a few days, you can still have the satisfaction of hosting a wonderful get-together.

We hope you will use *At Home with Friends* as a guide to bringing the ease and elegance of entertaining into your life. Our intention is to inspire you, and our goal is to bring families and friends together to enjoy good food and good company. Throughout, we have been careful to make simplicity the reigning principle. After all, the most important part of having people over is for you to enjoy your gathering as much as your guests do.

Of the many great things to do on a weekend, a leisurely breakfast is near the top of the list. A late Saturday or Sunday morning spent with good friends and a variety of good food is always a pleasure. Serve your late breakfast from about II A.M. until 2 P.M., and mix the sweet and hearty flavors of breakfast items with the salty and savory flavors of lunch.

BREAKFASTS

The sunny and casual character of breakfast is perfectly suited for celebrating special occasions. One of the simplest of parties to throw, it's ideal for a wedding or baby shower, birthday gatherings, and special anniversaries, and a traditional choice for holidays like Mother's Day, Father's Day, and Easter. Your guests are likely to have their mornings free, so scheduling is usually easier than with evening parties. Food is a breeze as well, as an assortment of fresh fruit, a savory baked dish or some bakery-fresh pastries, some juices, and good coffee make the meal.

Because of the simplicity of a breakfast, there's very little planning to be done. The first important decisions are the guest list and budget. If you're throwing a brunch in celebration of a shower, birthday, or some other special event, invitations may be in order. In this case, you'll want to buy or make invitations and allow time for mailing, and for guests to RSVP. If you're not sending invitations, it's a good idea to give guests a call at least a week in advance if the occasion is special. Your next important decision is where to put the guests and the food. If you're fortunate to have a garden or lawn, an outdoor breakfast on a warm morning is always a treat. If you're indoors, look for ways to bring a little of the outdoors in. Open the windows, bring in some flowers, and use sunny colors in your table settings.

With your guests invited, it's time to consider your menu. If you're pulling your party together at the last minute, keep it simple. In this case, we recommend mixing prepared foods with a couple of homemade dishes. For example, you might purchase bagels, lox, and cream cheese, then throw together a scramble of eggs, spinach, and sausage just before serving. Or, display granola, fresh berries, and yogurt on your buffet for your guests to serve themselves, followed by a delicious frittata straight from your oven. For a very special occasion, how about French toast or omelettes for those in a breakfast mood, and fresh vegetables and an assortment of breads and meats for those in the lunch state of mind? No matter what you serve, don't forget beverages. Mimosas and Bloody Marys are always popular at breakfast, as are fruit smoothies, espresso drinks, coffee, teas, fresh juices, and water.

When it comes time to serve your guests there are two ways to go: buffet style or seated. To decide which route to take, consider the number of guests you are hosting, the menu you are serving, and how much work you want to do. A buffet is by far the more popular choice. A buffet-style brunch works great for large groups, allows the hosts to truly enjoy their guests, and works well in most spaces, indoor or out (for more ideas on how to set up and decorate a buffet, see Chapter Four, "Buffets"). It's true that buffets put some limitations on your menu, as many breakfast dishes should be served piping hot. If you want to serve eggs or French toast, for example, you should choose a family-style, sit-down meal. If the guest list is on the shorter side, the family-style approach allows you to treat your company to beautiful table settings and exciting new recipes (see Chapter Three, "Dinner Parties," for tips on family-style meals). There's also the hybrid approach: a buffet with breads, granola, fruit, yogurt, and beverages, followed by pancakes, coffee cake, eggs, or ham straight from the oven.

The final step is to consider a few simple decorations. We recommend taking inspiration from the occasion you are celebrating or the menu you are serving. For example, a morning bridal shower buffet could be decorated with nothing more than simple white linens accented by small vases of flowers in the wedding's color theme. A sunny morning menu may feature freshly squeezed orange juice, so how about creating a centerpiece of citrus fruits piled into a compote, with linens in pastel yellow or white? No matter how you decorate, your décor needn't be fussy or complicated. Simple touches can make a big impact.

In this chapter, we present two unique breakfasts to inspire and guide you. The first, the Country Breakfast, is designed to be family style. We used color as our decorating theme, selecting linens in pale blue with silver accents and serving pieces. The French-Style Breakfast is served buffet style. Decorating inspiration comes from an outdoor setting, and the menu is a mix of purchased foods and home-cooked dishes.

savory breakfast bread pudding | blueberry-apricot muffins with
streusel topping | minted melon pearls | melon smoothies |
sourdough toast with mascarpone and berries | tea

COUNTRY BREAKFAST

ON THE MENU

If you have time, make this entire meal from scratch. If not, replace all of the recipes with our suggested prepared foods from your local market. Or, do a mix of the two. If you can, prepare a few things the night before so you will have more time to relax in the morning. The Savory Breakfast Bread Pudding is a good place to start. Slice up some day-old bread and let it dry overnight. In the morning, mix in the rest of the ingredients and pop it in the oven. Brew up a pot of herbal tea or make a batch of Melon Smoothies as your guests arrive. A basket of freshly baked (or fresh from your bakery) Blueberry-Apricot Muffins or a stack of toasted sourdough bread is an unexpected treat when accompanied with ripe berries, mascarpone, and honey. Melon is delicious tossed with a minted honey dressing—slice it into wedges or cubes or scoop into balls in a variety of sizes.

PLAN-AHEAD PARTY

TWO DAYS AHEAD	ONE DAY AHEAD	DAY OF THE PARTY	JUST BEFORE THE PARTY	DURING THE PARTY
• Decide on menu, review recipes and timesavers, and make shopping lists • Shop for groceries and any table decorations, fresh flowers, or fruit • Gather serving pieces, plates, linens, napkins, tableware, and so on; purchase any missing items	• Wash and prepare fruit for melon salad, smoothies, and muffins • Cube bread for bread pudding and leave out to dry overnight • Bake muffins	• Set up table or arrange seating area with tableware, centerpieces, linens, and so on	• Prepare bread pudding • Transfer honey and mascarpone to bowls or jars • Toss melon with dressing; add mint, and transfer to a serving bowl	• Brew coffee and tea; set out cream and sugar • Make smoothies • Toast bread

SERVING IT UP

If the weather is nice and you're lucky enough to have a garden, set up a table outside. An umbrella or overhead structure such as an arbor or a pergola can provide some shelter from the sun. Indoors, a sunny spot in the kitchen, dining room, or living room is ideal—set up a breakfast table or dining table, or place stools around a kitchen counter.

For a casual touch, choose a favorite tablecloth, runner, or place mats, or layer several pieces on top of each other to add texture. To create a more elegant setting, choose pieces from your china closet— a silver teapot, tray, platters, and bowls can easily mix with many styles of dinnerware, even simple white dishes. Don't worry about polishing—a little tarnish gives silver a lovely patina. If you have them, mix in a few natural elements like rattan, wicker, and bamboo; they combine well with silver, white, and cream for a casual elegance.

Make use of any pretty glassware you have in your collection, and don't be restricted by the rules. Melon Smoothies are just as appropriate in wineglasses as they are in tumblers, and even fancy cocktail glasses make spirited containers.

The finishing touch—a beautiful centerpiece—needn't be complicated or costly. Fill little silver, glass, or ceramic cups with a few blooms from your garden or your local flower shop. Lilacs, camellias, spring bulbs, roses, peonies, and flowering branches are all great choices. Give a pretty potted plant a temporary home on your breakfast table. A grouping of fresh fruit in a silver or ceramic bowl, tray, or platter is quick and elegant, and the perfume of ripe fruit will enhance any setting. For an extra-special occasion, carry the centerpiece theme a little further. Fold cloth or linen napkins, place them on each plate, and lay a fresh or silk flower, or even a pretty leaf, atop each one.

INSTANT PARTY

THE NIGHT BEFORE	DAY OF THE PARTY	JUST BEFORE THE PARTY	DURING THE PARTY
• Decide on menu, review timesavers, and make shopping lists • Shop for groceries and any table decorations, fresh flowers, or fruit • Gather serving pieces, plates, linens, napkins, tableware, and so on; purchase any missing items	• Set up table or arrange seating area with tableware, centerpieces, linens, and so on	• Warm quiche • Warm muffins or coffee cake • Transfer honey and mascarpone or ricotta to bowls or jars • Chill fruit juice • Transfer precut melon to bowl and add fresh mint	• Brew coffee and tea; set out cream and sugar • Toast bread • Pour fresh fruit juice or smoothies over crushed ice

SAVORY BREAKFAST BREAD PUDDING SERVES 6

1   *16-OUNCE LOAF DAY-OLD FRENCH BREAD, CRUST REMOVED, CUT INTO 1-INCH CUBES*

4   *OUNCES COOKED BREAKFAST SAUSAGE, CUT INTO $1/4$-INCH SLICES*

$1/2$ *YELLOW ONION, CHOPPED*

6   *EGGS*

1   *CUP HALF-AND-HALF OR WHOLE MILK*

2   *TABLESPOONS MINCED FRESH THYME*

$1/2$ *TEASPOON SALT*

$1/2$ *TEASPOON FRESHLY GROUND PEPPER*

This bread pudding is a delicious alternative to a pancake breakfast. While French toast, pancakes, and waffles must be made a few at a time, this dish bakes in a pan and is ready to serve to everyone at once. If you have time the night before, cube the French bread, slice the sausage, and chop the onion. In the morning, all you will need to do is to combine the ingredients and pop the pan into the oven.

Preheat the oven to 350°F. Coat a 10-inch pie pan with vegetable oil cooking spray. In a large bowl, combine the bread cubes, sausage, and onion. In a medium bowl, whisk the eggs, half-and-half or milk, thyme, salt, and pepper together. Pour the egg mixture over the bread mixture and stir to combine, making sure all the bread is thoroughly coated. Let sit for 10 minutes to absorb. Spoon into the prepared pan and bake for 30 to 35 minutes, or until top is crusty and golden brown.

TIMESAVER: Buy a fresh quiche from the bakery or deli, or a frozen one from the freezer section of the grocery store.

BLUEBERRY-APRICOT MUFFINS
WITH STREUSEL TOPPING MAKES 6 MUFFINS

STREUSEL TOPPING

2   TABLESPOONS CHILLED UNSALTED BUTTER

$^1/_3$ CUP PACKED LIGHT BROWN SUGAR

$^1/_3$ CUP BLANCHED ALMONDS, COARSELY GROUND

1   18-OUNCE BOX BLUEBERRY MUFFIN MIX, WITH
    CANNED {NOT DRIED} BLUEBERRIES

$^1/_2$ CUP DRIED APRICOTS, FINELY CHOPPED

$^1/_2$ CUP FRESH BLUEBERRIES

These charming little muffins are made from a commercial muffin mix. After selecting your favorite mix, make sure you have the ingredients it requires as well (usually one egg and water or milk, and sometimes vegetable oil). Reserve the canned blueberries that come with the mix for another use.

Preheat the oven to 425°F. Cut a piece of parchment paper into six strips, each 6 inches wide and 8 inches long. Fold the strips in half lengthwise, to make 3-by-8-inch strips. Wrap each strip into a 2-inch cylinder, tucking one end into the fold of the other end. Secure each cylinder with a piece of string. Line 6 muffin cups with paper baking cups and place a parchment cylinder in each one.

To make the topping: In a small bowl, combine all the ingredients. Stir until blended but still lumpy.

In a large bowl, combine the muffin mix with the apricots and fresh blueberries. Gently mix to separate the apricots, being careful not to break the berries. Combine the wet ingredients called for in the box instructions and fold into the blueberry mixture, mixing only until blended. The batter should be slightly lumpy. Fill the paper cylinders three-fourths full with batter. Halfway through baking, check cylinders and use your fingers to prop them up if they are leaning. Working quickly, top with the streusel and return the pan to the oven. Bake for about 20 minutes, or until lightly browned. Remove from the oven and let cool. Remove from the paper baking cups, retaining the parchment and string tie for serving.

TIMESAVER: Buy blueberry muffins or coffee cake from a bakery or grocery store.

MINTED MELON PEARLS SERVES 6

1   *HONEYDEW MELON, HALVED, SEEDED, AND CUT INTO QUARTERS*

1   *CANTALOUPE MELON, HALVED, SEEDED, AND CUT INTO QUARTERS*

$1/2$ CUP HONEY

$1/4$ CUP FRESH LIME JUICE

$1/4$ CUP CHOPPED FRESH MINT

This is a beautiful and simple way to serve melon. For a great look, use melon ballers in large, medium, and small sizes. It takes a little time to cut the melons into balls, but the effect is worth it.

Using a melon baller, cut balls from each melon, placing them in a large bowl as you work. Refrigerate the melon balls for at least 1 hour.

In a small bowl, combine the honey and lime juice. Stir until the honey dissolves, then add the mint. Pour over the chilled melon balls, toss, and serve.

TIMESAVER: Buy a ready-made melon or fruit salad from the grocery store.

MELON SMOOTHIES SERVES 6

6   *CUPS DICED HONEYDEW MELON*

$1/2$ CUP HONEY

JUICE OF TWO LIMES

ICE CUBES FOR BLENDING

This drink utilizes the same ingredients as the Minted Melon Pearls, making for easier shopping.

In a blender, combine half of the melon, $1/4$ cup honey, and half the lime juice. Fill with ice cubes and blend on high for 1 minute, or until ice is crushed. Serve immediately. Repeat with the remaining ingredients.

TIMESAVER: Substitute a good-quality, fresh fruit juice and serve over crushed ice or purchase prepared smoothies from a well-stocked market.

frittata française | potatoes lyonnaise with caramelized onions | provençal salad platter with herbed vinaigrette | brioche french toast with caramelized peaches | tangerine mimosas | chicken liver pâté with pistachios | the best café au lait

FRENCH-STYLE BREAKFAST

ON THE MENU

This versatile breakfast takes advantage of fresh ingredients and the rich culinary traditions of France. The menu takes its inspiration from a French cafe in New York City. While service there was admittedly terrible, the food and atmosphere couldn't have been more charming. The delicious, and uncomplicated, dishes translate perfectly for an at-home brunch.

As your guests arrive, start them off with café au lait made with equal portions of good strong coffee and hot milk, served the traditional way, in bowls. Fresh Tangerine Mimosas made with fresh ripe fruit and a little Champagne add a festive touch to any breakfast.

This menu has just the right balance of sweet and savory, beginning with the Brioche French Toast with Caramelized Peaches. If you have time the night before, get a head start by making the Potatoes Lyonnaise. Aside from being an excellent, hearty side dish, it is the perfect complement to many French dishes. You can also prepare the fresh vegetables for the salad platter and frittata. In the morning, whip up the simple tomato and chanterelle mushroom frittata and assemble the salad platter. Chicken liver pâté is a French classic and is available at most grocery stores and gourmet markets. Add some toasted pistachios to make it special. If you are lucky enough to have a French bakery in your neighborhood, pick up some of their specialties to add to your brunch: pastries, breads, and a few cookies or little cakes for dessert.

PLAN-AHEAD PARTY

TWO DAYS AHEAD	ONE DAY AHEAD	DAY OF THE PARTY	JUST BEFORE THE PARTY	DURING THE PARTY
• Decide on menu, review recipes and timesavers, and make shopping lists • Shop for groceries and any table decorations, fresh flowers, or fruit • Gather serving pieces, plates, linens, napkins, tableware, and so on; purchase any missing items	• Wash and prepare vegetables for salad platter, frittata, and Potatoes Lyonnaise • Make pâté • Make Potatoes Lyonnaise • Boil eggs and steam vegetables for salad platter; make vinaigrette • Set up table or arrange seating area with tableware, centerpieces, linens, and so on	• Make French toast and frittata; keep warm in oven • Make mimosas; chill juice and Champagne in an ice bucket or in refrigerator	• Assemble salad platter and transfer pâté to a serving dish • Brew coffee; set out cream, sugar, and café au lait condiments in containers	• Restock empty platters, brew more coffee, and refill empty condiment containers • Serve French toast and frittata • Clear plates and tidy up tables

SERVING IT UP

If the weather is nice, consider moving your breakfast outside. A large, shady tree, an umbrella, or a pergola is the perfect spot to pull up a table and set the meal up buffet style. Your guests can serve themselves throughout the party and find a comfortable place to linger on your patio or in your garden. Make available an assortment of places to sit—garden walls, folding and lounge chairs, even steps—if you don't have enough chairs. Bring cushions and throw pillows outside. A throw blanket and pillows set in a shady area of the lawn is a wonderful place for a picnic-style setup.

Perhaps you live in an apartment, with no access to a garden. You can simply create a sunny mood indoors with a few decorative touches. Pull out some bright-colored linens and tableware. Fresh colors like yellow, chartreuse, and orange look great mixed with white. Tablecloths, runners, napkins, and even dishcloths are quick and easy ways to add color and texture to your table, or use them to line trays and baskets. Simple white serving pieces and dinnerware are basic in most kitchens, so make use of what you have and mix and match with your color scheme. Use baskets, painted pots, metal trays and baskets, or colorful ceramics for serving. Group a stack of plates, a pile of napkins, flatware, and glasses on one end of the table. If you have a small side table or two, use it to serve the café au lait and tangerine mimosas. On a tray, set a carafe of freshly brewed espresso, a small pitcher of steamed milk, little bowls of sugar, vanilla, and bits of chocolate. Coffee cups, or small dessert or cereal bowls, can substitute for café au lait bowls if you don't have them.

Citrus fruits are an easy and inexpensive way to decorate a table. Pile lemons, oranges, tangerines and kumquats in a compote, tray, or platter. Add a few lemon leaves, usually available in the floral section of the grocery store, or pick some leaves from your trees in the garden. Extra citrus wrapped in a mesh, cellophane, or paper bag quickly tied with a piece of cording, ribbon, or twine makes a thoughtful gift for your guests to take home. If you've set the table for a sit-down brunch, use extra fruit to mark each place setting. Fold each napkin, set it on a plate, and place a lemon, an orange, or a few kumquats on top.

INSTANT PARTY

THE NIGHT BEFORE	DAY OF THE PARTY	JUST BEFORE PARTY	DURING THE PARTY
• Decide on menu, review recipes and timesavers, and make shopping lists • Shop for groceries and any table decorations, fresh flowers, or fruit • Gather serving pieces, plates, linens, napkins, tableware, and so on; purchase any missing items	• Assemble salad platter • Set up table or arrange seating area with tableware, centerpieces, linens, and so on	• Warm quiche or frittata; warm potatoes, or set out potato salad • Make French toast and keep warm in oven • Make mimosas; keep juice and Champagne in ice bucket or in refrigerator • Brew coffee; set out cream, sugar and café au lait condiments in containers • Transfer pâté to a serving dish	• Restock empty platters, brew more coffee, and refill empty condiment containers • Serve French toast and quiche or frittata • Clear plates and tidy up tables

FRITTATA FRANÇAISE serves 6

8   EGGS

3/4   CUP MILK

3   ROMA TOMATOES, SEEDED AND CHOPPED

8   OUNCES CHANTERELLE MUSHROOMS, CUT
    INTO QUARTERS

6   FRESH CHIVES, CHOPPED

1/2   TEASPOON SALT

1/2   TEASPOON GROUND PEPPER

1/2   CUP GRATED PARMESAN CHEESE

Chanterelle mushrooms, tomatoes, and chives add great flavor to simple scrambled eggs. If you can't find chanterelles, substitute another variety, such as shiitake or small brown cremini. Add 1/2 cup sliced prosciutto for a great boost of flavor.

Preheat the oven to 350°F. In a large bowl, whisk the eggs and milk together until well blended. Add the tomatoes, mushrooms, chives, salt, and pepper. Stir again. Spray a 9-by-12-inch baking pan with vegetable oil cooking spray. Pour the mixture into the pan and sprinkle the cheese evenly on top. Bake for 20 to 30 minutes, or until well browned.

TIMESAVER: Buy a fresh or frozen quiche or frittata from a bakery or gourmet market.

POTATOES LYONNAISE WITH
CARAMELIZED ONIONS _{SERVES 6}

2   *POUNDS POTATOES, PEELED AND QUARTERED*

2   *LARGE RED ONIONS, CUT INTO THIN SLICES*
    AND SEPARATED INTO RINGS

1   *TABLESPOON FRESH THYME*

1   *TABLESPOON FRESH ROSEMARY*

1   *TEASPOON SALT*

1   *TEASPOON GROUND WHITE PEPPER*

1/4 *CUP OLIVE OIL*

If baby potatoes can't be found, cut large potatoes into 3/4-inch cubes.

Preheat the oven to 350°F. In a large bowl, combine all the ingredients except the olive oil. Pour the oil over the ingredients and toss until well coated.

Transfer to a 9-by-13-inch baking dish and cover with aluminum foil. Bake for 30 to 40 minutes, or until well browned. Remove the foil and bake for 10 minutes longer, or until tender.

TIMESAVER: Buy frozen home-style potatoes (found premade in the freezer section of the grocery store) or potato salad from a deli or gourmet market.

PROVENÇAL SALAD PLATTER
WITH HERBED VINAIGRETTE SERVES 6 TO 8

VINAIGRETTE

- 2 *TABLESPOONS MINCED FRESH THYME*
- 2 *FRESH BASIL LEAVES, MINCED*
- 1 *TABLESPOON DRIED LAVENDER BLOSSOMS*
- 1/4 *CUP CHAMPAGNE VINEGAR*
- 3/4 *CUP GRAPESEED OIL*

  SALT AND FRESHLY GROUND WHITE PEPPER TO TASTE

SALAD

BUTTER LETTUCE LEAVES

ARUGULA

RADICCHIO LEAVES

ENDIVE LEAVES

TOMATOES, CUT INTO WEDGES

HARICOTS VERTS, BLANCHED FOR 3 TO 5 MINUTES

HARD-BOILED EGGS

BLACK OLIVES

JULIENNED CARROTS

BREAKFAST RADISHES

ASPARAGUS, BLANCHED FOR 3 TO 5 MINUTES

This toss-your-own salad offers something for everyone. Arrange a bountiful selection of salad ingredients on a large platter and invite your guests to mix and match their own salad to suit their tastes. The lavender-infused dressing is equally delicious as a marinade for pork, fish, or chicken.

Put the vinaigrette ingredients in a small bowl and whisk until combined. Cover and refrigerate for 1 hour.

Arrange the salad ingredients, or a selection of the salad ingredients, on a platter. Serve the dressing on the side.

TIMESAVERS: Buy a bottle of your favorite vinaigrette from your grocer. Buy bags of prepared lettuce, julienned carrots, pear or cherry tomatoes, and sliced radishes in the produce section of the grocery store.

BRIOCHE FRENCH TOAST WITH CARAMELIZED PEACHES SERVES 6

16   OUNCES SLICED FRESH PEACHES OR
      ONE 16-OUNCE PACKAGE FROZEN SLICED PEACHES

1/2 CUP SUGAR

1   TABLESPOON ALMOND EXTRACT

6   TABLESPOONS UNSALTED BUTTER, CUT UP,
      PLUS 2 TABLESPOONS

3   EGGS

1   CUP MILK

1   TEASPOON GROUND CINNAMON

6   INDIVIDUAL MUFFIN-SIZED BRIOCHES, HALVED
      LENGTHWISE

1/2 CUP SLICED ALMONDS, TOASTED {OPTIONAL}

This French toast is so good, you won't even need syrup. Look for brioche in your local French bakery or gourmet grocery store; substitute challah or sourdough bread if necessary. Apples, pears, or berries make great toppings if peaches are unavailable.

Preheat the oven to 450°F. In a 9-by-13-inch baking pan, combine the peaches, sugar, almond extract, and 6 tablespoons butter. Bake for 15 to 20 minutes, or until the peaches are lightly browned.

Put the remaining 2 tablespoons butter in a 4-by-8-inch nonstick loaf pan, and place in the oven for 10 minutes. In a shallow bowl, whisk the eggs, milk, and cinnamon together. Dip the brioche halves in the egg mixture and place, cut-side down, in the heated baking pan. Bake for 7 to 10 minutes, or until toasted on the bottom. Place the brioches on a platter toasted-side up and top with the caramelized peaches. Sprinkle with toasted almonds, if desired.

TIMESAVER: Substitute good-quality canned peaches.

CHAPTER ONE: BREAKFASTS

TANGERINE MIMOSAS SERVES 6

1   BOTTLE CHAMPAGNE OR SPARKLING WINE

4   CUPS TANGERINE OR BLOOD ORANGE JUICE, OR A COMBINATION

Tangerine or blood orange juice is a wonderful alternative to orange juice, especially in mimosas. For a nonalcoholic version, substitute flavored or plain sparkling water for the Champagne.

Refrigerate the juice and Champagne for 1 hour. Pour into a large pitcher and stir. Serve at once.

TIMESAVER: Buy freshly squeezed juice, concentrate, or bottles of tangerine juice at the grocery store.

CHICKEN LIVER PÂTÉ WITH PISTACHIOS SERVES 6

2   CUPS {8 OUNCES} PISTACHIO NUTS, CHOPPED

2   POUNDS CHICKEN LIVER PÂTÉ

Pâté is a delicious and unexpected addition to the breakfast table. Here, pistachios add color and crunch to an otherwise silky-smooth pâté. Serve with a good hearty bread from your local bakery.

In a medium skillet over medium heat, toast the pistachios for 3 to 4 minutes, or until fragrant. Pour into a medium bowl and let cool completely. Line a 4-by-8-inch loaf pan with plastic wrap. Press the pâté into the pan, filling in the corners. Smooth the top of the pâté. Remove the pâté from the pan and remove the plastic wrap. Roll the pâté in the nuts until it is completely coated. Refrigerate for 20 minutes. Serve with country bread and assorted crackers.

TIMESAVER: Omit the pistachio nuts and serve the pâté as is.

THE BEST CAFÉ AU LAIT ^{SERVES 6}

4$\frac{1}{2}$ CUPS WHOLE MILK

4$\frac{1}{2}$ CUPS FRESHLY BREWED COFFEE OR ESPRESSO

OPTIONAL CONDIMENTS

GROUND CINNAMON

VANILLA BEANS

SUGAR

UNSWEETENED COCOA POWDER

HONEY

ORANGE AND LEMON ZEST STRIPS

Here's a simple way to make the traditional cup of coffee or espresso infinitely more interesting. Your guests will be thrilled by the choices of your custom coffee bar. Stock your "bar" with traditional and unusual coffee condiments.

In a medium pan, heat the milk over low heat until bubbles form around the edge of the pan. Whisk to form frothy bubbles. In an insulated coffee carafe, combine the coffee and milk. Serve with the condiments.

TIMESAVER: Skip the orange and lemon zest and serve with flavored syrups.

Long, warm days and the smell of cut grass call for outdoor entertaining. Whether it's a casual weekend barbecue or a fabulous Fourth of July pool party, eating outside makes the simplest of meals into a true celebration.

OUTDOOR ENTERTAINING

Outdoor entertaining is perfect for groups of all sizes. The only limits to your planning are weather and space. A big backyard lends itself to a lazy afternoon barbecue, while a patio is a great place for a smaller affair. Choose the time of your party to correspond with the sun. If you live in a very hot climate, you'll want to opt for morning or evening, to avoid the hottest part of the day. Backyard parties are ideal for last-minute planners, as the casual barbecue requires far less planning than a sit-down meal or even a buffet. For those of us who don't have the luxury of a yard, grill pans have made grilling indoors an easy option. And a sunny kitchen or dining room is a fine substitute for a backyard.

Once you've picked a location for your party, it's time to decide on the menu. You may want to make use of an outdoor grill for chicken, burgers, steaks, or grilled vegetables, of course, but you can also prepare dishes inside and bring them out. You could diverge completely from the traditional barbecue fare and choose a culinary theme like a "Mediterranean" party, as we did with one menu in this chapter, featuring pizzas, mezes, and sangría. Cherry lemonade and citrus ice tea are nice variations on classic outdoor beverages. Whatever you choose to serve, try to select dishes that can be made in advance and served at room temperature, and those that can be store bought. Ideally, you want your preparation and hosting to be as carefree as your setting.

The easiest way to serve outdoors is buffet style. You can set up a buffet with nothing more than a card table and linens, or improvise on any surface available. Just be sure to choose an area away from direct sunlight and high traffic. If you want to add a flare to your buffet, tablecloths made from linen, cotton, or burlap look great outdoors, as do runners in patterned or woven fabrics. Enamelware is a good choice for outdoors, as is plastic tableware. Of course, paper cups and plastic utensils are probably easiest, especially with a big crowd. Be sure to have trash bags available for your guests. Finally, try bringing a bit of the outdoors to your buffet in the serving pieces you choose. For example, wooden cutting boards, slabs of stone, and galvanized buckets all make great serving pieces and maintain that rustic outdoor feeling. For more helpful hints setting up a buffet, see Chapter Four.

One of the best parts of entertaining outdoors is that there's very little decorating to do: The natural setting provides all the ambience you need. For a special occasion, a little attention paid to the buffet and guest tables goes a long way. It's best to go with simple ideas and bright colors that work in harmony with the outdoor setting. Try using patterned tablecloths on each table or even cover them in butcher paper. If your location is really bright, you may want to open up some patio umbrellas. And if you insist on going the extra mile by creating centerpieces, keep them simple. Buckets or wood crates full of fruit work well in an outdoor environment, as do small arrangements of wildflowers, or groupings of objects like bottles or candles. Speaking of candles, lighting is probably the most important design element for outdoor entertaining in the evening. Tiki torches, hanging lanterns, and candles create a magical setting. You can also trying floating candles in pools or stringing lights in trees. In fact, for night parties, great lighting is just about all the decorating you need.

In this chapter, we've designed two outdoor parties to inspire you and to provide you with new ideas and recipes. The first is a traditional barbecue with a ranch twist, with a menu that includes Grilled Tri-Tip with a Savory Dry Rub, Grilled Whole Chicken, Roasted Tomato and Onion Halves with Herb Marinade and Easy Apple Pie. The second is the Mediterranean Grill, with flavors of the sea in dishes like Grilled Whole Snapper with Grilled Lemon and Herbs, Couscous with Herbs and Grilled Octopus, and mezes, traditional Mediterranean appetizers.

grilled tri-tip with savory dry rub | grilled whole chicken | quick vegetarian black bean chili | roasted tomato and onion halves with herb marinade | simple slaw | easy apple pie | cherry lemonade | beer

RANCH-STYLE BARBECUE

ON THE MENU

Take advantage of fresh seasonal foods and open-air cooking for this casual barbecue. Because enthusiastic helpers abound at a grill party, it's easy to get friends involved with the preparation. Start with a big batch of Cherry Lemonade and serve it up as the guests arrive. Bottled beer and sodas on ice make it easy for guests to serve themselves. At center stage are the grilled meats. Dry rubs are one of the most flavorful and easiest ways to season poultry and beef for the grill. As the meat heats up, the juices combine with the herbs and seasonings to create a flavorful crust. Grilling whole chickens on open beer cans is an old trick and works really well for keeping them moist and juicy.

A trio of side dishes satisfies any vegetarian and makes a wonderful complement to grilled meat. The Simple Slaw is crispy and refreshing, a nice, light alternative to heavy salads. A lighter yet equally hearty and tasty variation on traditional chili is vegetarian chili made with black beans, peppers, and tomatoes. If you have any extra-ripe tomatoes, throw them on the grill with some onion halves and brush them with a delicious herb marinade while the meats are grilling. For dessert, nothing can beat apple pie. Make the pie early in the day or the night before and quickly reheat it on the grill before serving. A generous dollop of whipped cream or a scoop of vanilla ice cream is the perfect accompaniment.

PLAN-AHEAD PARTY

TWO DAYS AHEAD	ONE DAY AHEAD	DAY OF THE PARTY	JUST BEFORE THE PARTY	DURING THE PARTY
• Decide on menu, review recipes and timesavers, and make shopping lists; don't forget charcoal or propane	• Wash and prep vegetables; store in containers or bags in the refrigerator	• Set up a table with tableware, centerpieces, linens, lighting, and so on	• Transfer coleslaw and cherries to serving dishes, set out on table	• Restock ice bucket with drinks and refill Cherry Lemonade jar
• Shop for groceries and any table decorations, such as candles or fresh flowers	• Make chili	• Set up grilling area with a small table and grilling tools	• Reheat chili	• Grill the tri-tip, chicken, and tomato and onion halves; serve immediately
• Gather serving pieces, plates, linens, napkins, tableware, and so on; purchase any missing items	• Make herb marinade, marinate onions and tomatoes, and store in refrigerator	• Assemble coleslaw and refrigerate	• Light grill	• Heat pie; serve immediately
	• Marinate tri-tip and chicken with dry rub; store in refrigerator	• Make lemonade and chill drinks in refrigerator or an ice bucket		• Clear plates, remove empty wine bottles, and tidy up table
		• Assemble pie and refrigerate		

SERVING IT UP

First set up the barbecue and prep table, then focus on creating a comfortable space for your friends to relax and enjoy the day. If it's a daytime event, make sure to find plenty of shady seating. A patio overhang, pergola, large tree, and movable umbrellas are all good options. If your space is out in the open, you can fashion a colorful canopy from a tablecloth tied to poles stuck in the ground. Pull up patio furniture and bring additional furniture from inside the house to create an outdoor living area. Sturdy, casual furniture in wood or metal works well. Folding chairs, benches, and even cut tree trunks can be used around the party area for extra seating. Set up a picnic-style party on a shady lawn with floor cushions, throw blankets, and tablecloths.

For the eating area, cover a folding table with a patterned picnic blanket or tablecloth, letting it drape to the floor to hide the legs. Whether you set up buffet or sit-down style, you will need serving pieces and tableware to dish up the food. Clean painted buckets can hold a variety of things from cherries to coleslaw to napkins and utensils. Serve meats on wooden slabs or cutting boards. Metal trays, platters, and baskets are all useful for serving up side dishes and holding condiments. Cut sections of wood are a fun way to display plates of food. Use wood under bowls, buckets, and platters to give height and texture to the table. A stack of plates—enamel, metal, wicker picnic plate holders, or even simple everyday dishes—can be used outside. Sturdy glasses or jars for drinks can be grouped near a large glass canister or jug of Cherry Lemonade. Add a ladle so guests can easily help themselves. Stock plenty of bottled drinks in an ice bucket or two.

For a nighttime party, hang lanterns and torches around the party area; cluster hurricane lamps, candles, and votives on tables and around seating. String globe or tiny white lights through a patio awning or pergola for an overall glow. Build a crackling fire in an outdoor fireplace or fire pit.

INSTANT PARTY

THE NIGHT BEFORE

- *Decide on menu, review recipes and timesavers, and make shopping lists; don't forget charcoal or propane*
- *Shop for groceries and any table decorations such as candles, fruit, or flowers*
- *Gather serving pieces, plates, linens, napkins, tableware, and so on; purchase any missing items*

DAY OF THE PARTY

- *Set up a table with tableware, linens, lighting, and so on, and a grilling area with a small table and tools*
- *Wash and prep onions and tomatoes for roasting and marinate*
- *Chill lemonade and drinks in refrigerator or an ice bucket*

JUST BEFORE THE PARTY

- *Light grill*
- *Transfer coleslaw to a serving dish; set out on table*
- *Reheat chili or baked beans*
- *Reheat roasted chicken*

DURING THE PARTY

- *Refill wineglasses or restock ice bucket with drinks*
- *Grill tri-tip, tomato, and onion halves; serve immediately*
- *Heat pie; serve immediately*
- *Clear plates, remove empty wine bottles, and tidy up tables*

GRILLED TRI-TIP WITH
SAVORY DRY RUB SERVES 6 TO 8

SPICE RUB

2   TABLESPOONS MINCED GARLIC

2   TABLESPOONS MINCED FRESH ROSEMARY

2   TABLESPOONS GROUND CORIANDER

1   TABLESPOON SWEET HUNGARIAN PAPRIKA

1   TABLESPOON CELERY SEED

1   TABLESPOON GROUND MUSTARD

1   TABLESPOON CRACKED PEPPER

1   TABLESPOON KOSHER SALT

1   3-POUND TRI-TIP ROAST

2   TABLESPOONS OLIVE OIL

Tri-tip—also called Santa Maria tri-tip, or a bottom sirloin tip roast—is flavorful and easy to cook on the grill. We like to season the meat with a dry rub made with fresh herbs. There are several well-made commercial spice mixes on the market now; if you need to save time, purchase one, adding minced garlic and fresh herbs to it.

In a small bowl, combine all the ingredients for the rub. Mix until well blended. Place the roast on a cutting board, brush it with the olive oil, and rub the entire surface of the meat with the spice mixture. Wrap in plastic and refrigerate for at least 1 hour or up to 24 hours.

Prepare a medium-hot fire in a charcoal grill, or preheat a gas grill to medium-high. Place the roast on the center of the grill, cover the grill, and cook, turning once after 15 minutes, for a total of 30 minutes for medium rare. Remove from the grill and allow to rest 15 minutes before carving.

TIMESAVER: Buy a prepared dry rub.

GRILLED WHOLE CHICKEN SERVES 6 TO 8

SPICE RUB

1   *TABLESPOON GRATED LEMON ZEST*

1   *TABLESPOON MINCED FRESH THYME*

1   *TABLESPOON GROUND CUMIN*

1   *TEASPOON CHILI POWDER*

1   *TEASPOON GROUND ALLSPICE*

1   *TEASPOON GROUND CINNAMON*

1   *TEASPOON CRACKED PEPPER*

1   *TEASPOON KOSHER SALT*

1   *ROASTING CHICKEN, ABOUT 3 1/2 POUNDS*

1   *TABLESPOON OLIVE OIL*

1   *12-OUNCE CAN BEER OR LEMONADE*

This technique may sound odd, but the result is a plump, moist, very flavorful roasted chicken. Placing the bird over an open can of liquid (we like beer, but lemonade can also be used) also keeps the skin from burning before the inside is cooked. If your grill is large enough, you can save time by grilling this at the same time as the tri-tip roast.

In a small bowl, combine all the ingredients for the rub. Put the chicken on a cutting board. Run your fingers under the skin over the breast. Rub the olive oil under the skin and all over the surface of the skin, then do the same with the spice rub. Wrap in plastic and refrigerate for at least 1 hour or up to 1 day. Remove the chicken from the refrigerator 30 minutes before grilling.

Prepare a medium-hot indirect fire in a charcoal grill, or preheat a gas grill to medium-high. Open the beer or lemonade can and pour out one-third of the liquid. With the can standing upright, insert the can into the cavity of the chicken. Place the chicken and the can upright over indirect heat, cover, and grill for 1 hour, turning a one-quarter turn every 15 minutes. Remove from the grill and allow to rest 15 minutes before carving.

TIMESAVER: Buy roasted chickens in the deli section of a grocery store.

QUICK VEGETARIAN
BLACK BEAN CHILI SERVES 6 TO 8

3   TABLESPOONS OLIVE OIL

1   LARGE YELLOW ONION, CHOPPED

*1   LARGE YELLOW BELL PEPPER, SEEDED,
     DERIBBED, AND CUT INTO THIN
     LENGTHWISE STRIPS*

1   15-OUNCE CAN DICED TOMATOES, DRAINED

1   TABLESPOON GROUND CUMIN

1   TEASPOON SWEET HUNGARIAN PAPRIKA

1   TEASPOON CAYENNE PEPPER

1   TEASPOON DRIED OREGANO

1   TEASPOON KOSHER SALT

2   15-OUNCE CANS BLACK BEANS

*Using canned black beans makes this recipe a snap. Make   the flavor
time to mellow, and to give yourself more time on the da*

In a large pot, heat the olive oil over medium heat. Sauté the
Stir in the tomatoes, then stir in the cumin, paprika, cayenne, oregano, and sai
then add the black beans. Bring to a boil, reduce the heat, and simmer for 20 minutes. Let cool, cover,
refrigerate for 1 day. Reheat before serving.

TIMESAVER: Buy canned chili or baked beans at the grocery store or prepared chili from a takeout restaurant or deli.

ROASTED TOMATO AND ONION
HALVES WITH HERB MARINADE SERVES 6 TO 8

MARINADE

1/4 CUP SHERRY VINEGAR

1   TABLESPOON DIJON MUSTARD

1/2 TEASPOON KOSHER SALT

1/2 TEASPOON CRACKED PEPPER

1   TEASPOON MINCED FRESH THYME

1/2 CUP OLIVE OIL

4   LARGE, RIPE TOMATOES, HALVED CROSSWISE

4   YELLOW ONIONS, HALVED LENGTHWISE

Nearly any vegetable can be cooked on a grill. We've settled on two of our favorites. If you like, make a brush for applying the marinade by tying rosemary, thyme, and sage sprigs together. Not only is it practical, imparting flavor, but it is pretty, too.

To make the marinade: In a small bowl, combine the vinegar, mustard, salt, pepper, and thyme. Gradually whisk in the oil. Use now, or cover and refrigerate for up to 1 week.

Prepare a medium-hot indirect fire in a charcoal grill, or preheat a gas grill to medium-high. Brush the marinade over the cut sides of the tomatoes and onions.

Place the onions over indirect heat, cut-side down, for 8 to 10 minutes. Turn the onions over and add the tomatoes to the grill. Brush the onions again with the marinade and cook 8 to 10 minutes on the second side. Cook the tomatoes 3 to 4 minutes on each side, brushing again with the marinade after turning.

TIMESAVER: Buy your favorite bottled herb marinade.

CHAPTER TWO: OUTDOOR ENTERTAINING

SIMPLE SLAW SERVES 6 TO 8

DRESSING

1/4 CUP APPLE CIDER VINEGAR

1   TABLESPOON DIJON MUSTARD

1   TEASPOON CRACKED PEPPER

1/2 TEASPOON CELERY SALT

2   TABLESPOONS LOW-FAT MAYONNAISE

1/3 CUP CANOLA OIL

1/2 HEAD GREEN CABBAGE, CORED AND THINLY
     SLICED

1   YELLOW BELL PEPPER, SEEDED, DERIBBED,
     AND CUT INTO VERY THIN LENGTHWISE SLICES

6   GREEN ONIONS, INCLUDING GREEN PARTS,
     CUT LENGTHWISE INTO THIN 2-INCH STRIPS

This crisp, tangy side salad goes well with savory dishes and pairs perfectly with the grilled flavors in this chapter. If you are looking for a timesaver, skip the dressing step and buy a commercially made slaw dressing of your choice.

In small bowl, combine the vinegar, mustard, pepper, and celery salt. Whisk in the mayonnaise, then gradually whisk in the oil.

In a large bowl, toss the cabbage, bell pepper, and green onions together until mixed. Drizzle the dressing over all and toss again. Serve immediately.

TIMESAVER: Buy prepared coleslaw in the deli section of the grocery store or gourmet market, or buy a bag of prepared coleslaw ingredients in the produce section of the grocery store.

EASY APPLE PIE SERVES 6 TO 8

2   *LARGE GRANNY SMITH APPLES, PEELED, CORED,*
     AND CUT INTO $^1/_2$-INCH SLICES

1$^1/_2$ *CUPS FRESH CHERRIES, PITTED*

1   *CUP WALNUTS, COARSELY CHOPPED*

$^1/_4$ *CUP PLUS 1 TABLESPOON SUGAR*

2   *TABLESPOONS ALL-PURPOSE FLOUR*

2   *8-INCH COMMERCIAL REFRIGERATED PIECRUSTS*

2   *TABLESPOONS UNSALTED BUTTER, CUT INTO PIECES*

1   *EGG YOLK, BEATEN WITH 1 TABLESPOON WATER*

Commercial, refrigerated piecrusts are a perfectly acceptable option for a time-pressed host. Find them in the refrigerated section of your grocery store, usually where the biscuit and cookie doughs are kept. We've added cherries and walnuts, but the pie will be just as delicious without them. There's nothing like hot apple pie right out of the oven, but if necessary, you can make this the day before serving. If you do so, be sure to warm it for a few minutes on the grill or in the oven before serving. Serve with whipped cream alongside.

Preheat the oven to 400°F. Line a baking sheet with parchment paper. In a large bowl, toss the apples, cherries, and walnuts together. In a small bowl, mix the 1/4 cup sugar and the flour together until well combined. Sprinkle the sugar mixture over the apple mixture and toss again; set aside.

Remove the piecrusts from their pans. On a lightly floured board, press the crusts together and roll out to a diameter of 14 inches. Transfer to the prepared baking sheet. Put the apple mixture in the center of the dough and spread to a circle of about 10 inches in diameter. Scatter the butter pieces on top. Fold the edge of the piecrust dough up over the fruit, pleating as you go around the pie. Brush the crust edges with the egg mixture and sprinkle the remaining 1 tablespoon sugar over the crust. Bake for about 35 minutes, or until the crust is golden brown.

TIMESAVER: Buy apple, cherry, or berry pies from a bakery.

CHERRY LEMONADE SERVES 6 TO 8

2   *CUPS FRESH LEMON JUICE*

1   *CUP UNSWEETENED BOTTLED CHERRY JUICE*

1/2 *CUP SUGAR*

2   *QUARTS SPARKLING WATER*

Here's the quintessential summer beverage. Serve this colorful juice in a clear pitcher to show off its rosy hue. Add a few lemon slices and sprigs of fresh mint, if you like.

In a large pitcher, combine the lemon juice, cherry juice, and sugar. Add the sparkling water and stir until the sugar is dissolved. Taste and adjust the sweetness. Serve over ice.

TIMESAVER: Buy prepared lemonade at the grocery store.

CHAPTER TWO: OUTDOOR ENTERTAINING

meze platter | grilled squid and lemon skewers | mediterranean pizza | grilled whole snapper with grilled lemon and herbs | cucumber, tomato, and grilled octopus salad | couscous with herbs and grilled octopus | pistachio ice cream with crushed pistachios | white wine sangría

MEDITERRANEAN GRILL

ON THE MENU

If spending a relaxing day outside in the company of friends is on your entertaining wish list, this fun menu fits the bill. A fresh and flavorful Mediterranean grill is surprisingly easy to pull off, and a party based on these delicious foods is elegant and casual at the same time. A leisurely afternoon meal, Mediterranean style, is a perfect warm weather ritual for a birthday party, out-of-town houseguests, or a spontaneous dinner with friends.

Start the party by offering up a glass of refreshing White Wine Sangría. The light, fruity flavors complement a seafood menu perfectly.

Make a big batch and serve it in a large jar or glass canister so everyone can help themselves. An ice bucket filled with sparkling water, wines, and Greek beer offers alternatives. While the grill gets going, guests can snack on delicious appetizers. Mezes are the traditional start to a Mediterranean meal: trays and dishes of rustic breads, olives, pickled vegetables, goat cheese, crackers, tapenade, and an herb-infused olive oil for dipping.

A menu centered around fresh seafood is one your guests are sure to enjoy. A light combination of herbs and sea salt brings out the fresh flavors of the sea. Grill up a whole snapper or two by simply sealing them in aluminum foil and cooking them on the grill until the meat flakes off the bones. Traditional couscous gets a flavor infusion with another Mediterranean delicacy—octopus—and takes only a few minutes to make. Pizza topped with a light tomato sauce and fresh herbs cooks to a delicious smoky crunch on the grill.

End the meal on a sweet note and another flavor of the Mediterranean with bowls of creamy pistachio ice cream topped off with toasted pistachio nuts.

PLAN-AHEAD PARTY

TWO DAYS AHEAD	ONE DAY AHEAD	DAY OF THE PARTY	JUST BEFORE THE PARTY	DURING THE PARTY
• Decide on menu, review recipes and timesavers, and make shopping lists; don't forget the charcoal or propane • Shop for groceries and any table decorations, such as candles, fruit, or fresh flowers • Gather serving pieces, plates, linens, napkins, tableware, and so on; purchase any missing items	• Wash and prep vegetables; store in containers or bags in refrigerator • Make cucumber salad • Make sangría • Make tapenade	• Set up a table with tableware, centerpieces, linens, lighting, and so on • Set up grilling area with a small table and grilling tools • Assemble pizza • Thread octopus onto skewers; thread squid and lemon wedges onto skewers	• Make couscous and transfer cucumber salad to a serving dish • Assemble Meze Platter • Light the grill	• Refill sangría glasses and restock ice bucket with drinks • Grill snapper, octopus, squid and lemon skewers, and pizza; serve immediately • Clear plates, remove empty wine bottles, and tidy up tables • Toast pistachios and serve with ice cream

SERVING IT UP

Make a cozy floor space outside by layering a woven mat over a patio. Pull up an old weathered table and use it as a buffet, dining, or prep table. Then add a coffee table and some patio or rustic furniture, and you've created an intimate setting for your party.

Whether you set the table for a sit-down meal or serve the meal buffet style, there are many options for creating a beautiful look. A palette of ocean blues and pale stone mixed with red, orange, or yellow evokes the Mediterranean seaside. Use rustic materials mixed with bright colors on the table. Fold a piece of fabric and use it to layer the table. Bring out stoneware, ceramics, or vintage china and combine them with metal, wood, and stone. Depending on the mood you want to create, choose glassware to complement the look—everything from sturdy old jars to elegant stemware is right for sangría.

For a party that extends into the night, lanterns, string lights, and torches will keep the party going. On tables, group votives in glass jars and candles in hurricane lamps in clusters.

Arrange the meze platters so they become edible centerpieces. A weathered piece of stone or a wood cutting board can hold breads and crackers. Ceramic, metal, or wood bowls are perfect for nibbles like olives and pickled veggies, as well as condiments like tapenade and coarse salt. Pile a few extra lemons or limes in a bowl for color. Old stone or glass bottles make beautiful containers for olive oil, dipping sauce, and vinegar. Seaside treasures like shells and beach pebbles can be used on the table. For a sit-down meal, fold cloth napkins, set one on each plate, and hold them down with a little seashell or beach pebble.

INSTANT PARTY

THE NIGHT BEFORE

- *Decide on menu, review recipes and timesavers, and make shopping lists; don't forget the charcoal or propane*
- *Shop for groceries and any table decorations, such as candles, fruit, or fresh flowers*
- *Gather serving pieces, plates, linens, napkins, tableware, and so on; purchase any missing items*

DAY OF THE PARTY

- *Set up a table with tableware, linens, lighting, and so on, and a grilling area with a small table and grilling tools*
- *Assemble snapper in foil packets*
- *Thread octopus and squid and lemon wedges on skewers*

JUST BEFORE THE PARTY

- *Light grill*
- *Chill wine*
- *Make instant couscous and transfer cucumber salad to a serving dish*
- *Assemble Meze Platter*

DURING THE PARTY

- *Refill wine glasses and restock ice bucket with drinks*
- *Grill snapper, octopus, squid and lemon skewers, and pizza or focaccia; serve immediately*
- *Clear plates, remove empty wine bottles, and tidy up tables*
- *Toast pistachios and serve with ice cream*

MEZE PLATTER SERVES 6

FRESH TOMATO RELISH

3   *ROMA TOMATOES, CHOPPED*

2   *CLOVES GARLIC, CHOPPED*

3   *TABLESPOONS OLIVE OIL*

5   *LARGE FRESH BASIL LEAVES, CHOPPED*

3   *TABLESPOONS BALSAMIC VINEGAR*

1   *TEASPOON SUGAR*

TAPENADE

8   *OUNCES KALAMATA OLIVES, PITTED*

1/4 *CUP OLIVE OIL*

SLICES OF COUNTRY BREAD

The traditional meze platter is a simply prepared selection of Mediterranean appetizers. Your guests will enjoy the two spreads here served with nothing more than perfect, crusty bread. Or you can embellish the platter with bite-sized morsels of grilled vegetables, squid, or fish.

To make the relish: In a food processor, combine all the relish ingredients and pulse until coarsely chopped.

To make the tapenade: In a food processor, combine the olives and olive oil. Process to a coarse paste.

TIMESAVER: Purchase bottled tapenade and sun-dried tomato paste from your grocery.

GRILLED SQUID AND
LEMON SKEWERS SERVES 6

3   *TABLESPOONS OLIVE OIL*

1   *TEASPOON SALT*

1/2   *TEASPOON FRESHLY GROUND PEPPER*

2   *TABLESPOONS MINCED FRESH THYME*

1   *JAR ROASTED RED PEPPERS, CUT INTO*
    1-INCH-WIDE STRIPS

12   *SQUID, CLEANED*

3   *LEMONS, CUT INTO WEDGES*

The ultimate finger food, these skewers are easily assembled and cook in less than 15 minutes. Cleaned fresh or thawed frozen squid can be found at many markets.

Prepare a hot fire in a charcoal grill, or preheat gas grill to high. Soak 12 wooden skewers in water for 30 minutes; drain. In a small bowl combine the olive oil, salt, pepper, and thyme. Whisk to blend. Set aside. Roll up 1 or 2 red pepper strips and stuff into each squid body. Slide a stuffed squid onto each skewer, followed by 1 lemon wedge. Brush with the olive oil mixture. Grill for 5 to 10 minutes, or until opaque and lightly browned. Serve hot or at room temperature.

TIMESAVER: Buy premade marinade from the grocery store or gourmet market.

MEDITERRANEAN PIZZA SERVES 6

8 OUNCES PIZZA DOUGH

2 TABLESPOONS OLIVE OIL

1 6-OUNCE CAN PIZZA SAUCE

1 5-OUNCE JAR KALAMATA OLIVES

8 OUNCES GOAT CHEESE

1 EACH YELLOW AND RED BELL PEPPERS, SEEDED,
   DERIBBED, AND CUT INTO 1/2-INCH CHUNKS

OPTIONAL TOPPINGS

3 BABY ARTICHOKES, COOKED AND QUARTERED

1/2 RED ONION, CUT INTO WEDGES

1 CUP {4 OUNCES} SHREDDED SMOKED GOUDA

4 OUNCES PORTOBELLO MUSHROOMS, SLICED

8 OUNCES BRIE CHEESE

Whether made in the oven or on the grill, this pizza is quick, easy, and colorful. Choose your favorites from the selection of toppings, or present a variety and invite guests to create their own pizzas before popping them on the grill.

Prepare a hot fire in a charcoal grill, or preheat a gas grill to high. On a lightly floured board, roll the dough out into an oblong circle about 12 inches long and 9 inches wide. Brush with the olive oil and prick all over with a fork. Place on a sheet of aluminum foil and place on the grill. Cover the grill and bake for 15 minutes, or until the crust is golden brown. Open the grill and sprinkle the pizza sauce evenly over the dough. Place the olives, goat cheese, bell peppers, and optional toppings on the pizza. Cover the grill and cook until the cheese is melted and toppings are cooked, about 20 minutes.

TIMESAVER: Substitute frozen pizza from the grocery store or gourmet market, or purchase a good focaccia with toppings from your local bakery.

GRILLED WHOLE SNAPPER WITH GRILLED LEMON AND HERBS _{SERVES 6}

2   *2-POUND WHOLE RED SNAPPERS*

2   *TABLESPOONS OLIVE OIL*

2   *TEASPOONS SALT*

1   *TEASPOON GROUND WHITE PEPPER*

6   *CLOVES GARLIC*

1   *BUNCH FRESH THYME*

1   *BUNCH FRESH TARRAGON*

1   *BUNCH FRESH MARJORAM*

1   *BUNCH FRESH DILL*

2   *LEMONS, HALVED*

Grilling is the perfect way to cook fish, and this simple dish lets the delicate flavors of fresh snapper shine through. If the snapper selection is less than ideal, you can substitute sea bass, halibut, trout, salmon, or another favorite fish. Just buy the freshest fish possible.

Prepare a hot fire in a charcoal grill, or preheat a gas grill to high. Put 1 fish on a piece of aluminum foil and brush with 1 tablespoon of the olive oil. Sprinkle with 1 teaspoon salt and 1/2 teaspoon white pepper, top with half of the garlic cloves, thyme sprigs, tarragon sprigs, marjoram sprigs, and dill sprigs. Squeeze half of a lemon over the fish. Repeat with the second fish. Fold the foil over the fish and crimp the edges closed. Put the packets on the grill, away from direct flame, and cook for 15 to 20 minutes. Open the foil and cook for another 8 to 10 minutes. Cut the remaining lemon into 1/4-inch-thick slices and grill for 2 minutes on each side. Serve the fish straight from the grill, garnished with the grilled lemon slices.

TIMESAVER: Buy an herb or citrus marinade at a grocery store.

CUCUMBER, TOMATO, AND GRILLED OCTOPUS SALAD SERVES 6 TO 8

2   ENGLISH {HOTHOUSE} CUCUMBERS, CUT INTO
SMALL CHUNKS

1   POUND CHERRY TOMATOES

8   OUNCES FETA CHEESE, CRUMBLED

    SEA SALT AND FRESHLY GROUND PEPPER TO TASTE

$1/_2$ CUP OLIVE OIL

$1/_4$ CUP BALSAMIC VINEGAR

8   OUNCES CLEANED OCTOPUS TENTACLES

In Greece, a cucumber, tomato, and feta cheese salad is a standard accompaniment to most meals. The addition of octopus, shrimp, or scallops makes it a complete entrée when served with crusty bread. This salad can be made up to 8 hours in advance and refrigerated.

Soak 2 long wooden skewers in water for 30 minutes. Prepare a hot fire in a charcoal grill, or preheat a gas grill to high. In a large bowl, combine the cucumbers, tomatoes, cheese, salt, and pepper. In a small bowl, whisk the oil and vinegar together. Pour over the salad and toss. Set aside.

Thread the octopus on the skewers and grill for 3 to 5 minutes, or until opaque and firm to the touch. Cool for 10 to 15 minutes, slice crosswise into thin circles, and mix into the salad. Garnish with fresh pepper.

TIMESAVER: Buy a cucumber salad from a Greek deli or gourmet market.

COUSCOUS WITH HERBS
AND GRILLED OCTOPUS _{SERVES 6}

2   *CUPS COUSCOUS*

1/2 *TEASPOON OLIVE OIL*

2   *TABLESPOONS FRESH THYME*

2   *TABLESPOONS FRESH MINT*

  SALT TO TASTE

4   *OUNCES CLEANED OCTOPUS TENTACLES*

A staple of the Moroccan and North African diet, couscous has become increasingly popular through-out the world, and no wonder. Not only does it cook up quickly, but it tastes great at any temperature. If you have trouble finding octopus, substitute grilled shrimp, scallops, or fresh tuna, or treat your guests to a combination of all three.

Soak 2 long wooden skewers in water for 30 minutes. Prepare a hot fire in a charcoal grill, or preheat a gas grill to high. Line a steamer basket with cheesecloth, add the couscous, and submerge in water for 5 minutes. Set the basket over a pot of boiling water, cover, and steam for 3 to 4 minutes. Rinse the couscous and continue to steam for 5 minutes. Fluff with a fork. Empty into a bowl. Add the olive oil, herbs, and salt and toss to mix. Set aside.

Thread the octopus tentacles on the skewers and grill for 3 to 5 minutes, until opaque or firm to the touch. Let cool 10 to 15 minutes and slice crosswise into circles. Garnish the couscous with the grilled octopus.

TIMESAVER: Buy a box of instant couscous from the grocery store and follow the cooking directions.

PISTACHIO ICE CREAM WITH CRUSHED PISTACHIOS SERVES 6

1   CUP {4 OUNCES} UNSALTED SKINNED PISTACHIOS

1   QUART PISTACHIO ICE CREAM

When you are in a hurry, this simple dessert does the trick. For best results, use premium ice cream and whole pistachios. Toasted cashew nuts with vanilla ice cream is another delicious variation.

In a skillet over medium heat, toast the nuts for 2 to 3 minutes, or until fragrant. Watch carefully to prevent scorching. Scoop the ice cream into a bowl. Top with the toasted nuts.

WHITE WINE SANGRÍA SERVES 6 TO 8

1   *BOTTLE {750 ML} DRY WHITE WINE*

4   *CUPS FRESH STRAWBERRIES, HALVED*

5   *ORANGES, SLICED*

2   *LEMONS, SLICED*

    ICE CUBES

1/2 *LARGE {1L} BOTTLE SPARKLING WATER*

Sangría is virtually foolproof. Give yours a personal touch with your favorite fruits and wine. Change the flavor by substituting ginger ale for the sparkling water, or adding freshly chopped mint.

In a large pitcher, combine the wine, fruit, and ice cubes. Top off with sparkling water.

TIMESAVER: Serve a Mediterranean wine instead of sangría.

A group of friends or family gathered around the dinner table always makes for a special occasion. The dinner party—perhaps the most traditional and popular form of entertaining—lends itself equally well to birthday or holiday meals and casual get-togethers with friends. Sit-down dinners can be as intimate and relaxed or as festive and lively as you wish. Some of the best dinners are made up of simple dishes prepared with a minimal amount of equipment and effort. And while a well-planned dinner calls for some attention to timing and detail, it needn't be labor intensive. A bit of forethought and some special touches will make your dinner party memorable.

DINNER PARTIES

Your first consideration for a sit-down meal is table space and seating. Start by choosing where you would like to serve your dinner. If you have a dining room, your work is done. If not, there are plenty of ways to accommodate a group of people. Try pushing two or more tables together. Folding tables, outdoor tables, picnic tables, or just about any flat surface you can hide under a tablecloth will also work. With the table in place, gather chairs from around the house, mixing and matching until you have the right number. Desk chairs, folding chairs, outdoor chairs, and even benches are fine. Armchairs will work in a pinch; just be sure to use them at the ends of the table. If you have a long coffee table, seat guests Japanese style on floor pillows or tatami mats.

Once you have figured out how to accommodate your guests, consider your kitchen space. Most people have one oven and four burners, so the order in which you prepare your dishes will be critical. You'll also need to make sure that you have enough pots, pans, dishes, and serving pieces. If you want to do all the cooking yourself, prepare as much as you can ahead of time and reheat the food dishes in the oven just before serving. If you're pressed for time, lighten your workload with prepared foods from gourmet grocers or local restaurants. Assemble a wonderful feast entirely with prepared foods, or augment one or two homemade entrees with an assortment of purchased sides and salads.

Using your menu as a springboard, consider a few simple decorations to accent your table setting. If you've chosen an ethnic culinary theme, take inspiration from that culture. Other sources of inspiration are the season, a holiday, or the colors of the food. Whatever you decide, begin by dressing the table. For formal dinners, linen or fine fabric tablecloths are customary. For more casual affairs, placemats add instant texture and visual interest. Fabric runners brighten the length of the table. For informal dinners, it's best to keep your place settings simple. Combine everyday white dishes with serving pieces from other patterns. A single plate will do, and tumblers are as good for wine as for water. If you want formal place settings, you'll need a dinner plate and a salad plate, and perhaps a soup bowl and spoon. Consider your beverages as well, and put out water and wine stemware as necessary.

A crowning addition to your table is a beautiful centerpiece. Food makes for great edible focal points: An arrangement of breads, olive oils, and dipping sauces create delectable centerpieces, as do pretty bowls overflowing with fruits or vegetables. Simple floral arrangements are another good option; try a single tropical leaf in an old glass bottle, herbs in a vase, or a cluster of flowers from your garden or your nearest store. A more formal dinner might call for a tray of lit candles, or flowers afloat in glass bowls of water. If flowers are a must for your party and you're short on time, splurge on an arrangement from a nearby florist. In any case, remember that the simplest centerpieces are the most striking. A fussy, overly cluttered table makes passing dishes and relaxing during the meal difficult. And be sure to keep all arrangements low and full so your guests can see one another.

You're likely to be busy in the kitchen when your first guests arrive, so ask a good friend or two to come over an hour or so early. An extra person can help with last-minute cooking, run out for that forgotten ingredient, greet guests, take jackets, and offer drinks. It's a good idea to have a simple appetizer or two out in the living room, along with a couple of open bottles of wine and some glasses. Guests can help themselves, and you'll breathe easily as you work on finishing touches in your kitchen.

While dinner parties are great for celebrating special occasions, they're also easy enough for a spontaneous gathering. The parties in this chapter, a Simple Family Dinner and an Asian Dinner, are distinctly different. Yet both use simple recipes, easy decorations, and fresh ideas to make a memorable evening.

white bean salad | orecchiette with butternut squash | roast
pork loin with sage and lavender | roasted root vegetables |
cannoli with orange zest | rustic breads | red wine

SIMPLE FAMILY DINNER

ON THE MENU

This updated home-style menu keeps preparation to a minimum, so you can spend more time enjoying the party with your guests. Easy enough to whip together at the last minute, this menu is equally perfect for a Friday night gathering or an early Sunday dinner. Either way, you'll be able to relax and enjoy the meal along with your guests.

A family-style dinner is the perfect opportunity to get guests involved. Instead of herding everyone out of the kitchen, let some of the guests help with the salad and lighter fare. Set out some bottles of wine, glasses, and a corkscrew, and your friends will feel right at home. On a section of the kitchen counter, make a grouping of rustic breads on a cutting board with a bread knife; add a bowl or two of olives or some other nibbles, a favorite dipping sauce or olive oil, and maybe a wedge of Parmesan.

Before your guests arrive, prepare the vegetables and pork loin so they can roast in the oven, creating wonderful scents of lavender and sage throughout the house. (If there are vegetarians in the group, make sure to roast the vegetables separately from the pork loin.) Once the entrée is in the oven, turn your attention to the salad and pasta. Vary the menu depending on your own tastes. For a small or impromptu gathering, you might want to eliminate the pasta and add a simple green salad. Consider adding a favorite chutney like mango or apricot for the pork loin. Once the roast comes out of the oven, wrap the bread in foil and pop it in the oven to warm while the pork loin rests. An updated classic of orange-flavored cannoli with a pot of decaffeinated Italian roast coffee is the perfect way to end the meal.

PLAN-AHEAD PARTY

TWO DAYS AHEAD	ONE DAY AHEAD	DAY OF THE PARTY	JUST BEFORE THE PARTY	DURING THE PARTY
• Decide on menu, review recipes and timesavers, and make shopping lists	• Wash and prep all vegetables; store in containers or bags in refrigerator	• Chill wine and drinks in refrigerator or ice bucket	• Begin roasting root vegetables and pork loin	• Refill wineglasses or restock ice bucket with drinks
• Shop for groceries and any table decorations, such as candles or fresh flowers	• Steam butternut squash and make pasta sauce; refrigerate	• Set up dinner table with place settings, centerpieces, linens, and chairs	• Set out breads, cheeses, wine, dipping sauce, and so on, in kitchen or seating area	• Cook pasta and finish making sauce
• Gather serving pieces, plates, linens, napkins, tableware, and so on; purchase any missing items	• Rub pork loin with herbs and refrigerate	• If your guests will help prepare the meal, set up prep space	• Fill a pot with water for boiling pasta	• Clear plates, remove empty wine bottles, and tidy up tables
		• Make white bean salad; refrigerate	• Remove white bean salad from refrigerator	• Whip cream for cannoli and fill shells

SERVING IT UP

The easiest way to serve a meal is family style from platters passed around the table. If room on the table is scarce, place the platters on a small table or sideboard near the dining table once the dishes have been passed. For a very large group of people, consider having two of everything, so that the passing can happen in double time. For smaller groups, plate the food in the kitchen and bring it out to the table—this is an especially good option for hosts with limited table space.

There are plenty of options when it comes to setting the table, and you can make it as simple or elaborate as the occasion calls for. Whether you choose a scrap of fabric to fold into a runner, an heirloom tablecloth, or woven placemats, choose a color palette that works with the decor and theme of the menu. You can layer a textured runner or place mats over a plain table or a covered one. A large tablecloth (long enough to cover the table and reach to the floor on all sides) is the perfect cover for a folding table. If you don't have one long enough, use a few small ones instead. Or, tape fabric or tablecloths around the table, first covering the sides down to the floor, then drape another cloth over the top to cover up the taped areas. Cloth napkins, simply folded or rolled and tied with a piece of twine or ribbon, are a nice touch.

Pull items from around your house; use things picked up from your travels. Mix and match vintage and heirloom pieces, or keep it simple with plain white dinnerware. Glassware doesn't have to be fancy, and tumblers can double as water glasses and wineglasses. Even the simplest of table settings can be special when wine is served in a carafe. Serve the food on platters, bowls, and trays—whatever you have in your collection. Bread can be simply placed on a wooden cutting board with a knife, or set inside a basket or container lined with a cloth napkin or clean dish towel. Small bowls can hold everything from sauces to chutney and olives. Group smaller bowls filled with coarse salt, freshly ground pepper, and fresh herbs on a pretty tray or platter.

A centerpiece of fresh fruit, such as pears, apples, or lemons clustered in a compote, tray, or platter, makes a colorful and easy display. Since everyone looks great in candlelight, create a relaxed mood by mixing candlesticks and skinny tapers with thick pillar candles and votives of different heights in a monochromatic color scheme for a glowing table. Grouping small clusters of flowers cut from the garden or purchased at the market and placed in little vases or cups looks great dotted down the center of the table or floating in a bowl.

INSTANT PARTY

THE NIGHT BEFORE	DAY OF THE PARTY	JUST BEFORE THE PARTY	DURING THE PARTY
• Decide on menu, review recipes and timesavers, and make shopping lists	• Arrange furniture and centerpieces; set up dinner table	• Begin roasting root vegetables and pork loin	• Refill wineglasses or restock ice bucket with drinks
• Shop for groceries, baked goods, prepared foods, fresh flowers, and so on	• Chill wine and drinks in an ice bucket or refrigerator	• Set out breads, cheeses, wine, dipping sauce, and so on, in kitchen or seating area	• Scoop vanilla ice cream and serve immediately with biscotti
• Gather serving pieces, plates, linens, napkins, tableware, and so on; purchase any missing items	• Rub pork loin with herbes de Provence	• If guests will help prepare the meal, set up prep space	• Clear plates, remove empty wine bottles, and tidy up tables
	• Place white bean salad in serving bowl; refrigerate	• Remove white bean salad from refrigerator	
		• Make green salad or reheat garlic mashed potatoes	

WHITE BEAN SALAD SERVES 6

3   15-OUNCE CANS CANNELLINI BEANS, DRAINED
     AND RINSED

1/2 CUP OLIVE OIL

1   BUNCH BASIL, STEMMED AND CHOPPED

     LEAVES FROM 1/2 BUNCH OREGANO, CHOPPED

     SALT AND FRESHLY GROUND PEPPER TO TASTE

Canned beans help this pretty salad come together quickly. Make the dish ahead of time—it tastes even better when the flavors are given time to meld. Substitute black-eyed peas, navy beans, or lima beans for the cannellini beans if desired.

In a large bowl, combine all the ingredients and mix well. Serve now, or cover and refrigerate for up to 24 hours. Bring to room temperature to serve.

TIMESAVER: Purchase bean salad at a gourmet grocery.

ORECCHIETTE WITH BUTTERNUT SQUASH SERVES 6

2   TABLESPOONS OLIVE OIL

2   POUNDS BUTTERNUT SQUASH, PEELED,
     SEEDED, AND CUT INTO 1-INCH PIECES

1   WHITE ONION, CHOPPED

3/4 CUP DRY WHITE WINE

4   CUPS CHICKEN STOCK OR CANNED LOW-SALT
     CHICKEN BROTH

     SALT AND FRESHLY GROUND PEPPER TO TASTE

1   POUND ORECCHIETTE

2   CUPS PACKED FRESH SPINACH LEAVES

¹/₂ CUP GRATED PARMESAN CHEESE

This comforting dish pairs pasta with a sweet and savory sauce of tender butternut squash and wine. If you can't find orecchiette ("little ears"), substitute penne, spaghetti, or even cheese-filled tortellini and ravioli.

In a medium saucepan, heat the oil over medium heat and sauté the squash and onion for 5 minutes, or until the onion is tender. Stir in the wine and cook for 1 minute. Stir in the stock or broth, and simmer for 20 to 30 minutes, or until the squash is tender and the liquid is reduced by one-fourth. Season with salt and pepper. Remove from heat and keep warm.

Cook the pasta in a large pot of salted boiling water until al dente, 9 to 10 minutes. Drain. Add the spinach to the squash mixture and cook over medium heat 1 to 2 minutes. Add the pasta and cheese, stir well until melted, and serve.

TIMESAVERS: Skip the pasta and serve the dinner with a green salad and extra bread, or serve garlic mashed potatoes from a gourmet shop or deli.

ROAST PORK LOIN WITH SAGE AND LAVENDER SERVES 6

3   *POUNDS BONELESS PORK LOIN ROAST, TIED*
    FOR ROASTING

2   *TABLESPOONS OLIVE OIL*

    SALT AND FRESHLY GROUND PEPPER TO TASTE

1   *BUNCH SAGE, CHOPPED*

2   *TABLESPOONS LAVENDER*

    CHERRY SAUCE {RECIPE FOLLOWS}, OPTIONAL

This hearty, herb-infused roast is sure to satisfy even the pickiest of eaters. Roasting is one of the easiest ways to cook meat. Ask your butcher to tie the pork loin for you.

Preheat the oven to 350°F. Rub the pork loin all over with the olive oil, then salt and pepper, then the herbs. Place in a roasting pan and roast for 1 hour, or until an instant-read thermometer inserted in the center registers 145°F. Remove from the oven and transfer to a platter. Cover loosely with aluminum foil and let rest for 15 minutes before slicing. Serve with cherry sauce on the side, if desired.

TIMESAVER: Purchase herbes de Provence from your grocer to use in place of the sage and lavender.

CHERRY SAUCE MAKES 1 CUP

2   *CUPS BOTTLED CHERRY JUICE*

1/2 *CUP DRIED CHERRIES*

This simple reduction of cherry juice studded with dried cherries takes just a few minutes to prepare.

In a small saucepan, bring the cherry juice to a boil. Reduce heat to a simmer; add the dried cherries, and cook to reduce the juice by half. Serve hot.

TIMESAVER: Purchase prepared cherry sauce from a well-stocked market.

CHAPTER THREE: DINNER PARTIES

ROASTED ROOT VEGETABLES SERVES 6

1   *BUNCH BABY CARROTS, TOPPED*

1   *BUNCH PARSNIPS, PEELED*

1   *BUNCH GREEN ONIONS*

1   *POUND FINGERLING POTATOES*

1/2   *CUP OLIVE OIL*

    SEA SALT AND FRESHLY GROUND PEPPER TO TASTE

Roasted vegetables are the natural accompaniment to roasted meat. Most vegetables, especially root vegetables, respond excellently to roasting, which caramelizes their natural sugars. For added flavor, use a large roasting pan and roast your meat and your vegetables together. For vegetarian guests, roast some vegetables separately.

Preheat the oven to 350°F. In a medium bowl, toss all the ingredients together. Spread in a roasting pan and cook for 1 hour, or until tender.

TIMESAVER: Buy prewashed and prepped vegetables like baby carrots and pearl onions, or substitute thick-sliced sweet potatoes.

CANNOLI WITH ORANGE ZEST <small>SERVES 6</small>

FILLING

15 OUNCES RICOTTA CHEESE, DRAINED

$^1/_4$ CUP GOLDEN RAISINS

$^1/_4$ CUP PISTACHIO NUTS

2-3 TABLESPOONS SUGAR

1 TABLESPOON GRATED ORANGE ZEST

6 CANNOLI SHELLS

This classic Italian dessert is unbelievably easy to make when you use purchased cannoli shells from an Italian bakery or well-stocked market. Replace the orange zest with lemon zest or $^1/2$ teaspoon of anise extract for interesting flavor twists. Use more or less sugar as you prefer.

In a medium bowl, combine all the filling ingredients. Blend well. Spoon the filling into the cannoli shells.

TIMESAVER: Substitute biscotti and vanilla ice cream.

CHAPTER THREE: DINNER PARTIES

asian crudités | crispy salmon spring rolls | sesame-crusted ahi | wasabi dipping sauce | ginger-scallion dipping sauce | ginger-shrimp dumplings | assembly-style soup | blood-orange cups | wine | beer | sake

ASIAN DINNER

ON THE MENU

This Asian dinner is the perfect solution for a special occasion. Whether it's an intimate holiday get-together, a birthday celebration, or a Friday night with friends, this is one of the most versatile and festive of parties. The menu is designed to be made completely ahead of time so that the host can enjoy the party as soon as guests arrive. Sake and beer start off the party in style. For an easy and sophisticated cocktail, mix one-part pineapple juice and one-part ice-cold sake.

A selection of Asian Crudités serves as an informal first course at the table, or they can be set out as hors d'oeuvres. The meal gets going with a mixture of savory small plates. Sesame-Crusted Ahi is quickly seared and topped with a tangy salad of sweet onions and ginger. Steamed Ginger-Shrimp Dumplings and Crispy Salmon Spring Rolls can be made ahead and reheated just before serving. A dipping sauce is quick to prepare, or you can substitute a favorite store-bought version. For the main course, an assembly-style soup is simple to make and easy to serve. Prepare the ingredients ahead of time and arrange on a serving platter or tray to store in the refrigerator. The broth can be left to simmer on the stove top until dinnertime. Guests can create their own custom soup by choosing their favorite ingredients from the platter. For dessert, a sectioned blood orange is the ultimate in elegance and simplicity.

PLAN-AHEAD PARTY

TWO DAYS AHEAD	ONE DAY AHEAD	DAY OF THE PARTY	JUST BEFORE THE PARTY	DURING THE PARTY
• *Decide on menu, review recipes and timesavers, and make a shopping list* • *Shop for groceries and any table decorations, such as candles or fresh flowers* • *Gather serving pieces, plates, linens, napkins, tableware, and so on; purchase any missing items.* • *Wash, prep, and/or steam vegetables for crudités and soup; store in containers or bags in refrigerator*	• *Set up dinner table with place settings, centerpiece, linens, seating, and lighting* • *Cook shrimp and reserve some for soup; make dumplings* • *Prepare salmon rolls and refrigerate* • *Make Wasabi Dipping Sauce*	• *Chill wine and drinks in refrigerator or ice bucket* • *Prepare chicken for soup platter* • *Make soup and assemble greens and vegetables for soup on platter* • *If your guests will help prepare meal, set up prep space* • *Prepare blood oranges* • *Make seared ahi and arrange on a plate with dipping sauce*	• *Arrange crudités platter and set it out on table* • *Heat or reheat soup* • *Cook salmon rolls and reheat shrimp dumplings* • *Set up drink area*	• *Restock ice bucket with drinks* • *Add chicken and shrimp to soup platter and set out on table* • *After guests have chosen ingredients for their soup, ladle hot broth into their bowls* • *Clear plates, remove empty bottles, and tidy up tables*

SERVING IT UP

The traditional way to serve a Japanese meal is from a low table surrounded by seat cushions. It's easy to create this setting in your home using a coffee table and some throw pillows. A door or piece of wood can be converted into a low table set atop crates or cinder blocks. Cover with fabric or a tablecloth that reaches to the floor, or give the covering a fitted look by taping or stapling the fabric to the underside of the tabletop. The throw pillows don't have to match. The mood is festive, and comfortable.

Set up a self-service drink table in the living room so guests can help themselves during the party. An ice bucket filled with bottled drinks can be set on the floor next to the table within easy reach. Make sure to have necessities such as a corkscrew, bottle opener, glasses, napkins, garnishes, and even a small trash can nearby to keep the area tidy.

Choose one or two appetizers to serve before dinner; set them out on a coffee or console table in the living room so guests can nibble while they drink.

Bamboo, wood, ceramics, and glass are lovely decorative elements for an Asian table. Place mats can be linked together to make a runner, and wooden trays and bamboo containers are perfect for table decorations, centerpieces, and serving platters.

Keep hot appetizers like Ginger-Shrimp Dumplings and Crispy Salmon Spring Rolls hot by serving them directly from the bamboo steamers they are cooked in. Have plenty of small bowls on hand for dipping sauces and condiments. Because the menu doesn't require full place sittings, there are many options for dinnerware. A bowl for the soup, a small plate for the appetizers, and a little cup, bowl, or plate for the dessert is all you'll need. Drinks can be served in cordial, shot, or wineglasses, small tumblers, or sake cups. Roll napkins and secure with lengths of ribbon or cord, and tuck a flower into each.

Camellias, orchids, dahlias, ranunculus, peonies and roses all look wonderful floating in bowls filled with water. Cluster votives on small trays or placemats for soft lighting. Hang festive paper lanterns over the dinner table. They can be lit with lights made especially for them, or just hung from fishing line, wire, or string.

INSTANT PARTY

THE NIGHT BEFORE

- Decide on menu, review recipes and timesavers, and make shopping lists
- Shop for groceries, prepared foods, and any table decorations such as candles or fresh flowers
- Gather serving pieces, plates, linens, napkins, tableware, and so on; purchase any missing items

DAY OF THE PARTY

- Set up dinner table with place settings, centerpiece, linens, seating, and lighting
- Chill wine and drinks in refrigerator or in ice bucket
- If your guests will help prepare the meal, set up prep space
- Prepare soup broth and cook vegetables

JUST BEFORE THE PARTY

- Reheat spring rolls and shrimp dumplings
- Reheat soup broth and assemble shrimp, greens, and vegetables for soup on a platter
- Set up drink area
- Steam edamame, sprinkle with coarse salt, and place in serving bowl
- Arrange sushi and dipping sauce on a platter

DURING THE PARTY

- Restock ice bucket with drinks
- After guests have chosen ingredients for their soup, ladle hot broth into their bowls
- Clear plates, remove empty bottles, and tidy up tables
- Serve orange or pineapple sorbet

ASIAN CRUDITÉS <small>SERVES 6</small>

10   *OUNCES CHINESE LONG BEANS OR GREEN BEANS,*
TRIMMED AND CUT INTO 6- TO 8-INCH PIECES

8   *OUNCES SNOW PEAS, TRIMMED*

1   *DAIKON RADISH, PEELED*

1   *DOZEN QUAIL EGGS*

1   *BUNCH CARROTS, TRIMMED, PEELED, AND CUT*
INTO QUARTERS LENGTHWISE

4   *OUNCES ENOKI MUSHROOMS, OR*
4 OUNCES SHIITAKE OR WHITE MUSHROOMS,
QUARTERED {STEM SHIITAKES}

PLUM SAUCE OR BLACK BEAN SAUCE FOR DIPPING

This crudités platter is a welcome change from the standard carrot sticks and dip. Guests can use their fingers to pick up some pieces, but you should have some chopsticks on hand for the smallest foods. Add your favorite bottled Asian sauce for dipping.

Cook the beans in a large pot of boiling water for 3 minutes. Drain and plunge into a bowl of ice water to stop the cooking. Repeat the process for the snow peas, but cook for only 1 minute. Using a spiral slicer or a mandoline, cut the daikon into long, thin pieces. Refresh the daikon in a bowl of ice water to crisp it. Put the quail eggs in a small saucepan. Add water to cover. Bring to a boil and cook for 3 minutes. Cover and remove from the heat. Let cool for about an hour, or drain and run cold water over the eggs several times, then peel the eggs. Arrange the beans, snow peas, carrots, and mushrooms on a large platter, using the daikon as a "nest" for the eggs. Place a small bowl of sauce on the platter for dipping.

TIMESAVER: Purchase fresh or frozen edamame from the grocery store, steam, and serve sprinkled with coarse salt.

CRISPY SALMON
SPRING ROLLS MAKES 24 PIECES

8   *OUNCES THIN SALMON FILLET, PIN BONES AND
     SKIN REMOVED*

3   *GREEN ONIONS, GREEN PARTS ONLY, CUT INTO
     2-INCH SECTIONS*

1   *PACKAGE SQUARE WONTON SKINS*

1   *EGG WHITE, BEATEN WITH 1 TABLESPOON WATER*

     CANOLA OIL

*These delicious rolls can be assembled early in the day, then cooked just before your guests arrive.
They make a dramatic presentation if cut on a diagonal before serving.*

Cut the salmon fillet lengthwise into 2-inch-wide sections. Cut each section crosswise into 1/2-inch-wide
slices. You should have at least 12 slices. Cut the 2-inch sections of green onion into thin lengthwise strips.
Place a wonton skin on a work surface with one corner facing you in a diamond shape. In the lower third
of the diamond, place 4 or 5 onion strips, and top with 1 slice of salmon. Fold the lower point of the
diamond up over the filling and fold in the 2 sides. Brush the top of the diamond with the egg white
mixture and finish rolling up. Place, seam-side down, on a small platter. Continue with the remaining wonton
skins, salmon, and onions. Cover the platter with plastic wrap and refrigerate until the guests arrive.

In a medium nonstick skillet, heat 1 tablespoon of the oil over medium heat. Place 4 salmon rolls in pan
and cook, turning frequently for 4 minutes, or until evenly browned. Transfer to a platter and keep warm.
Repeat to cook the remaining rolls, adding more oil as necessary. Slice in half diagonally to serve.

TIMESAVER: Purchase spring rolls from an Asian restaurant.

SESAME-CRUSTED AHI MAKES ABOUT 24 PIECES

3   GREEN ONIONS, GREEN PARTS ONLY

$1/4$ CUP MIXED BLACK AND WHITE SESAME SEEDS

8   OUNCES AHI TUNA, CUT INTO 1-BY-5-INCH SLICES

2   TABLESPOONS PEANUT OIL

4   OUNCES WASABI PASTE

1   CUCUMBER, CUT INTO $1/4$-INCH-THICK SLICES

     WASABI DIPPING SAUCE {RECIPE FOLLOWS}

Crusted and seared ahi tuna combines a flavorful smokiness with the delicate quality of sushi. Prepare the vegetables and sear the ahi early in the day, refrigerate them separately, then assemble just before your guests arrive.

Cut the green onions into 3-inch lengths, then cut the lengths into very thin strips. Place in a small bowl of ice water until curled, about 20 minutes.

Place the sesame seeds on a plate. Roll the tuna pieces in the sesame seeds, coating completely on all sides. In a large nonstick skillet, heat the oil over high heat. Sear the tuna for about 30 seconds on each side. Remove using a slotted spatula, transfer to paper towels to drain, and cool completely. Slice crosswise into 1/2-inch-thick pieces.

To assemble, place a small amount of wasabi paste on each cucumber round. Place a piece of seared ahi on the wasabi, then top with a few strips of curled green onion. Serve with the dipping sauce.

TIMESAVER: Purchase sashimi or sushi from a Japanese restaurant or gourmet grocery store.

WASABI DIPPING SAUCE _{MAKES ABOUT 1/2 CUP}

$1/4$ CUP LOW-SODIUM SOY SAUCE

$1/4$ CUP SEASONED RICE VINEGAR

2 TABLESPOONS WASABI, OR MORE OR LESS TO TASTE

Wasabi is a brightly colored paste made of green horseradish. Found in Asian markets or in the Asian section of many supermarkets, it's the classic accompaniment to sushi. You can make this sauce more or less potent by increasing or decreasing the amount of wasabi paste in the recipe. Simplify the recipe even more by using a purchased sauce and adding wasabi to taste.

In a small bowl, combine the soy sauce, vinegar, and wasabi. Stir well to dissolve the wasabi.

TIMESAVER: Purchase dipping sauce at a gourmet store.

GINGER-SCALLION DIPPING SAUCE _{MAKES ABOUT 1/3 CUP}

$1/4$ CUP SOY SAUCE

$1/4$ CUP RICE VINEGAR

2 TABLESPOONS CHOPPED GREEN ONION

1 TABLESPOON GINGER, PEELED AND MINCED

This classic dipping sauce can be made ahead of time and stored in the refrigerator. It's the perfect accompaniment to the Ginger-Shrimp Dumplings on page 102.

In a small bowl, combine all the ingredients.

TIMESAVER: Purchase dipping sauce at a gourmet store.

GINGER-SHRIMP
DUMPLINGS MAKES ABOUT 24 DUMPLINGS

1   *PACKAGE ROUND WONTON SKINS*

1   *3-INCH PIECE FRESH GINGER, PEELED AND MINCED*

1/2   *CUP FINELY DICED CARROT*

4   *OUNCES MEDIUM SHRIMP, COOKED AND CUT*
     INTO 1/2-INCH PIECES

1   *EGG WHITE, BEATEN LIGHTLY*

2   *TABLESPOONS CANOLA OIL*

1/2   *CUP WATER*

     GINGER-SCALLION DIPPING SAUCE {PAGE 101}

These tender, gingery dumplings benefit from a cooking process that includes both pan-searing and steaming. Assemble the dumplings ahead of time and cook them as your guests arrive. The fresh flavor will be worth it.

Place a wonton skin on a work surface. Put a few pieces of ginger, carrot, and shrimp (about 1 tablespoon total) in the center of the skin, brush the edges lightly with the egg white, then fold in half, crimping the edges to seal. Repeat to use all the remaining filling and skins. Cover with plastic wrap and refrigerate until ready to cook.

In a large nonstick skillet, heat 1 tablespoon of the oil over medium-high heat. Place half the dumplings in the pan, sealed-edges up, and brown for about 4 minutes, adjusting the heat to keep them from burning. Pour 1/4 cup of the water into the pan, cover, reduce the heat to low, and steam for about 6 minutes. Repeat the process to cook the remaining dumplings. Serve with dipping sauce.

TIMESAVER: Purchase shrimp dumplings from an Asian restaurant, or buy frozen dumplings from a grocery store or Asian market.

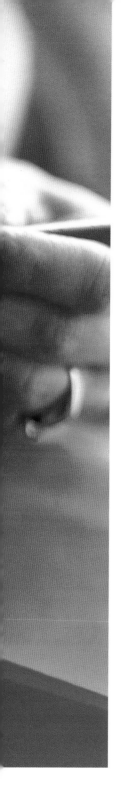

ASSEMBLY-STYLE SOUP ^{SERVES 6}

3	TABLESPOONS CANOLA OIL
3	BONELESS, SKINLESS SINGLE CHICKEN BREASTS, 6 TO 8 OUNCES EACH
1	POUND DRIED CHINESE EGG NOODLES
6	BABY BOK CHOY, HALVED LENGTHWISE
1	HEAD OF BROCCOLI, CUT INTO SMALL FLORETS
8	OUNCES SNOW PEAS, STEMMED AND CUT INTO $1/2$-INCH PIECES
8	OUNCES SHIITAKE MUSHROOMS, STEMMED AND THINLY SLICED
1	CUP SHREDDED CARROT
1	CUP THINLY SLICED GREEN ONION
8	OUNCES FIRM TOFU, CUT INTO $1/2$-INCH DICE
8	CUPS CANNED LOW-SALT CHICKEN BROTH

This main course is a lot of fun. Place a large platter of ingredients in the middle of the table and let your guests select the combination of ingredients they like in their bowl. Ladle hot broth over the ingredients, and the dish is done.

Heat 1 tablespoon of the oil in a medium nonstick skillet over medium heat. Sauté the chicken breasts, turning occasionally, until opaque throughout, about 12 minutes. Remove from the heat and let cool. Tear or chop into bite-sized pieces. Set aside.

In a large pot of boiling water, cook the noodles until tender, about 10 minutes. Drain, rinse with cold water, and toss lightly with the remaining oil. Set aside.

In another pot of boiling water, blanch the baby bok choy for 2 minutes, then drain and rinse with cold water. Repeat with the broccoli, cooking for 5 minutes. Repeat with the snow peas, cooking for 1 minute.

On a large platter, arrange the chicken, noodles, bok choy, broccoli, snow peas, mushrooms, carrot, green onion, and tofu in bowls or mounds. Wrap with plastic and refrigerate until ready to serve, up to 4 hours. Remove from the refrigerator 30 minutes before serving. In a large pot, heat the chicken broth until boiling. Ladle over the ingredients in each guest's bowl, or pour into a tureen and place on the table neat the platter of food.

TIMESAVER: Buy prepared vegetables and substitute cooked shrimp for the chicken.

BLOOD-ORANGE CUPS SERVES 6

3   *BLOOD ORANGES*

3   *TEASPOONS SUGAR*

This is a very easy, light dessert. With some simple cutting, the rinds of the oranges become pretty cups for the flesh. We like to use blood oranges when they are in season because they are so colorful, but navel oranges will work just as well. You'll need an orange for every two guests, but it's a good idea to buy an extra orange to practice on. Be sure to use a good, sharp knife.

Cut thin disks from the top and bottom ends of an orange and set the disks of rind aside. Cut the orange in half crosswise. Take one orange half and run the knife between the flesh and the rind, cutting right through to the bottom. Remove the flesh from the rind and set aside. You should have a ring of rind remaining. Place one reserved disk of rind inside (cut-side up) to form a bottom for the orange cup. Repeat to make the remaining orange cups.

Separate reserved orange flesh into segments by cutting along the sides of the membranes. Replace the segments in their orange cups, simulating the original look of the orange half.

Sprinkle each orange cup with 1/2 teaspoon sugar. Place on a platter, wrap in plastic, and refrigerate until ready to serve, or up to 4 hours. Serve chilled or at room temperature.

TIMESAVER: Serve an orange or pineapple sorbet.

CHAPTER FOUR

The simplest of all parties to host is the buffet. Whether for breakfast, lunch, or dinner, indoors or outdoors, a buffet can be set out at the last minute, with impressive results. Of the many reasons to choose a buffet, the foremost is the ease of planning and preparation. Beyond that, versatility, flexibility, and uncomplicated serving make the buffet a favorite way of entertaining friends.

BUFFETS

A buffet allows your guests to enjoy a full spread without the formality of a sit-down meal. You don't need to fit people around a table, fuss with place settings, or strategize about who sits next to whom. For anyone short on table space, seating, or serving pieces, the buffet is the perfect party. It allows you to freely mix and match your tableware, or to borrow from friends as need be. If you're lacking table space, just about any flat surface can become a useful buffet with the addition of a tablecloth or, in a pinch, a sheet. If you're short on seating, arrange stools and chairs from all the rooms in the house, or cluster some floor pillows away from foot traffic. If you don't have matching serving pieces, improvise; try displaying your food on any combination of cake stands, footed bowls, cutting boards, or trays.

Planning a buffet begins with the menu. It's a good idea to choose a general culinary theme, and build your menu around one main dish supported by complementary dishes. Consider how the flavors work together, and be sure to offer light as well as substantial fare. Since your food will be sitting out for a while, choose dishes that will not get soggy or dry, or unpleasant looking over time. If you don't have seating for each guest, choose food that is easy to eat, and plan on having the meal fit on one plate. If you're serving hot dishes, you'll need to consider timing. Plan your buffet so that you can bring out the hot dishes once all your guests have arrived.

In organizing your buffet, there are a number of ways to make your life easier. Just because you're the host doesn't mean you have to do all the work. Most guests offer to bring something, and it's perfectly appropriate to take them up on it. Bread, wine, cheeses, olives, fruits, and other ready-to-eat foods are good suggestions. And if you're short a few serving bowls, by all means borrow them. Also, don't shy away from serving already prepared food from a good specialty grocery store, deli, or bakery. And don't forget that you can always order from your favorite restaurants. If you decide to do a lot of the cooking yourself, choose dishes that you can make in advance and reheat just before the party. Mixing a few home-cooked dishes with some store-bought ones is a good way to maintain a personal touch while keeping preparation at a minimum.

When it comes to setting up your buffet, there are a few key principles to keep in mind. First and foremost, consider the flow of your traffic. Place the buffet in an area where many people can access it at once. Stack plates, flatware, and napkins all together at the starting end of the buffet so guests can easily find the essentials before moving on to the food. For large groups, it's a good idea to make your buffet accessible from both ends, each side with its own dishes, flatware, napkins, and food. Whatever the menu, be sure to include drinks. If there isn't enough room on the food table, place beverages and glassware on a separate table or counter near the main table. It's also a good idea to have a large pitcher of water and water glasses available. All the forethought will make your life much easier, as you won't have to fetch and arrange things while the party is in full swing.

Since we all eat with our eyes, it's important to make your buffet look appealing. When presenting your food, try to use serving pieces of varying heights and dimensions. This will create a more attractive arrangement and may even help to save table space, especially if you have footed bowls or cake stands. Color is the most important element in creating a beautiful buffet, adding visual interest and helping to pull the table together. You can choose your colors from your party's theme or take inspiration from the menu you've created; just be sure to keep it simple. Once you've decided your color theme, try to carry it into as many elements as possible.

Thoroughly versatile and modern, buffets can range from a casual afternoon of tasty snacks and drinks to an opulent display of luxurious dinner foods. In this chapter, you'll find two very different buffet parties. Whether you choose to make the dishes yourself or buy them already prepared, the buffet format will leave you free to enjoy your own party, your friends, and the bounty of food on your table.

great combos | vegetable platter | assortment of deli meats | selection of cheeses | assortment of breads | sandwich spreads & condiments | rare roast beef | roast turkey breast | oven-dried tomatoes | pan-roasted onions | arugula-jalapeño mayonnaise | roasted garlic spread | sweet potato oven fries | roasted tomato-garlic soup | onion-fennel soup | florentine sandwich cookies | beer | soda

A SOUP & SANDWICH BUFFET

ON THE MENU

This soup and sandwich buffet can be dressed up for an evening meal in celebration of a birthday, or kept picnic-casual for a New Year's Day or housewarming party. Buffets, particularly sandwich buffets, can be made completely portable for a day at the beach or an evening concert.

Whatever the occasion, it's easy to customize this buffet menu to create whatever kind of party you want. A late lunch or movie-night buffet calls for a lighter touch, while a Super Bowl party or a picnic supper demands heartier fare. Create a menu around a culinary theme—a gourmet French *dejeuner*, for example. Plan the menu to play up the theme, using lots of wonderful French cheeses, meats, breads, condiments like Dijon mustard, fresh herbs, cornichons, classic French onion soup, and of course, bottles of French wine. For a quick light lunch with a small group of friends, skip the sandwiches and serve just the soup with a selection of condiments, a fresh loaf of bread, and a tossed green salad.

You can easily update a classic like soup and sandwiches by introducing unusual ingredients and creating unexpected combinations. To build your sandwich buffet, start with the essentials—meats, cheeses, and breads—and provide a full range of flavors. Goat cheeses, Münster,

and roast turkey are excellent choices on the lighter side, while prosciutto, salami, and Cheddar have richer flavors, and a little will go a long way on a sandwich.

The vegetable platter is a must-have for vegetarian guests and an easy way to keep the menu on the light side. The classic standbys, lettuce and tomato, are essential. But your buffet can easily go gourmet with a few unusual additions—oven-dried tomatoes, roasted red peppers, spicy arugula. Everyone loves condiments, and they are a great way to add variety to the table. The condiments you serve should depend largely on your choices from the other categories.

Adding a wonderful soup or two and an assortment of side dishes takes the sandwich buffet to a new level of elegance. Just a few additions will allow you to feed more people and make your buffet more interesting. Turn a classic soup like roasted tomato into something extraordinary by offering a selection of condiments and toppers. Instead of greasy potato chips, try a healthy and easy side dish of roasted sweet potato fries. Bottled sodas, beer, and water are self-service in a nearby ice bucket, and chocolatey Florentine sandwich cookies are a perfect way to end the party.

PLAN-AHEAD PARTY

TWO DAYS AHEAD	ONE DAY AHEAD	DAY OF THE PARTY	JUST BEFORE THE PARTY	DURING THE PARTY
• *Decide on menu, review recipes and timesavers, and make shopping lists* • *Shop for groceries* • *Gather serving pieces, plates, linens, napkins, tableware, and so on; purchase any missing items*	• *Arrange furniture and set up a buffet table with tableware, serving pieces, flatware, and so on* • *Roast onions, tomatoes, and garlic; refrigerate* • *Make soups; refrigerate* • *Wash and prep vegetables; store in containers or bags in refrigerator* • *Make sandwich cookies*	• *Make Sweet Potato Oven Fries* • *Chill drinks in an ice bucket* • *Prepare roast beef and turkey breast* • *Slice cheeses, bread, and meats, if desired*	• *Heat soups and transfer to tabletop heaters, if desired* • *Arrange vegetables, cheeses, breads, and meats on serving dishes; set out on buffet table* • *Place condiments in small containers and arrange on buffet*	• *Restock empty platters and condiment bowls* • *Refill ice bucket with drinks* • *Clear plates, remove empty bottles, and tidy up the buffet table*

SERVING IT UP

Using the menu and number of people as a guide to help you create a beautiful buffet is easy. Once you've decided on the location, you can set up the buffet area. Tables can be covered with tablecloths, runners, or even a length of butcher paper. Basics like wooden cutting boards, dish towels, baskets, trays, and parchment paper are all useful serving pieces. If you're short on the essentials, wrap a scrap piece of wood with a clean sheet of parchment and you'll have a great-looking platter or tray. Line the inside of metal trays, baskets, or wicker picnic plate holders with parchment paper to use them as trays or plates.

Once you've gathered your equipment, concentrate on arranging the food on the serving pieces. Keep it organized by having separate serving pieces for each type of food: meats, cheeses, vegetables, and side dishes. Group each type of food together on the serving piece and place items with different colors and textures next to each other to create a beautiful display. If you are short on time, consider setting up a few cutting boards for whole meats, cheeses, and breads so guests can serve themselves. If you'd like to serve some things presliced, save time by having it done at the deli when you purchase your meats and cheeses. Soft cheeses and spreads are best served whole, with a spreading knife. Combine whole loaves of bread with sliced loaves, and individual baguettes. Use an assortment of little dishes, bowls, metal containers, and so on—anything you have around—for condiments, spreads, and nibbles.

Keep soup simmering in pots on the stove and create a mini buffet with condiments nearby, or hook up a couple of electric hotplates and place the soups directly on the buffet table. Serve soup condiments in small bowls or plates, grouping them on a tray near the soups. Fries or chips work well when served from a parchment- or napkin-lined basket, or create traditional paper cones filled with individual portions.

INSTANT PARTY

THE NIGHT BEFORE	DAY OF THE PARTY	JUST BEFORE THE PARTY	DURING THE PARTY
• *Decide on menu, review recipes and timesavers, make shopping list* • *Shop for groceries, baked goods, prepared foods, and so on* • *Gather serving pieces, plates, napkins, tableware, and so on; purchase any missing items*	• *Arrange furniture and set up buffet* • *Chill drinks in bucket or refrigerator*	• *Arrange breads, meats, cheeses, vegetables, and potato chips on buffet* • *Transfer condiments and spreads into small bowls and arrange on buffet* • *Reheat soup in pots on stove*	• *Restock empty platters, bread basket, soup pots, chips, and condiment bowls* • *Refill bucket with drinks* • *Clear plates, remove empty bottles, and tidy up the buffet table* • *Serve cookies*

GREAT COMBOS

- *BACON, ARUGULA, OVEN-DRIED TOMATO, AND AVOCADO, WITH A CREAMY HERB SPREAD ON SOURDOUGH*

- *TURKEY, MÜNSTER CHEESE, LETTUCE, ROASTED ONION, AND TOMATO, WITH FLAVORED MAYONNAISE ON RUSTIC COUNTRY BREAD*

- *ROAST BEEF, ARUGULA, ROASTED ONIONS, AND ROASTED PEPPERS, WITH HORSERADISH MAYONNAISE ON A BAGUETTE*

- *PROSCIUTTO, BRIE, AND ARUGULA, WITH ROASTED GARLIC SPREAD ON BAGUETTE*

- *SWISS CHEESE, LETTUCE, SPROUTS, TOMATO, AND AVOCADO, WITH TAPENADE ON SOURDOUGH*

- *SALAMI, PARMESAN, AND ROASTED PEPPERS, WITH OLIVE PASTE ON ROASTED GARLIC BREAD*

These are just a few of our favorite sandwich combinations. Make sandwiches ahead of time and serve them on a buffet, or pack them in a picnic basket for a portable party.

VEGETABLE PLATTER

(ALLOW 1 TO 2 SERVINGS OF EACH VEGETABLE PER PERSON)

SLICED TOMATOES	*SPROUTS*
OVEN-DRIED TOMATOES	*AVOCADO, SLICED OR MASHED {SQUEEZE SOME*
ROASTED ONIONS	*FRESH LEMON JUICE OVER THE TOP TO PREVENT*
	IT FROM TURNING BROWN}
LETTUCES	*ROASTED PEPPERS*

TIMESAVERS: Purchase prewashed lettuce—everything from romaine hearts to mixed baby greens, arugula, and baby spinach leaves. Substitute commercial guacamole for the avocado. Buy jarred peppers or purchase pepper salad from a deli.

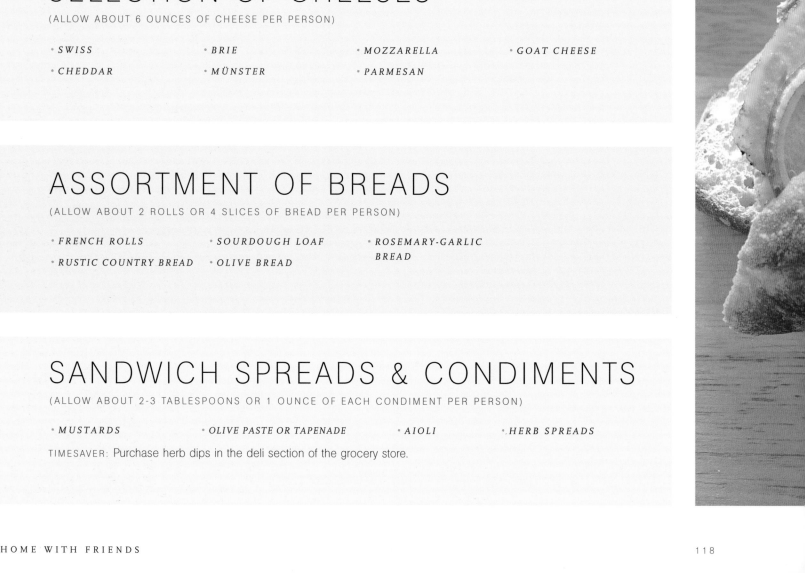

ASSORTMENT OF DELI MEATS

(ALLOW ABOUT 6 OUNCES OF MEAT PER PERSON)

- *PROSCIUTTO*
- *SALAMI*
- *BACON*
- *RARE ROAST BEEF*
- *ROAST TURKEY BREAST*

SELECTION OF CHEESES

(ALLOW ABOUT 6 OUNCES OF CHEESE PER PERSON)

- *SWISS*
- *CHEDDAR*
- *BRIE*
- *MÜNSTER*
- *MOZZARELLA*
- *PARMESAN*
- *GOAT CHEESE*

ASSORTMENT OF BREADS

(ALLOW ABOUT 2 ROLLS OR 4 SLICES OF BREAD PER PERSON)

- *FRENCH ROLLS*
- *RUSTIC COUNTRY BREAD*
- *SOURDOUGH LOAF*
- *OLIVE BREAD*
- *ROSEMARY-GARLIC BREAD*

SANDWICH SPREADS & CONDIMENTS

(ALLOW ABOUT 2-3 TABLESPOONS OR 1 OUNCE OF EACH CONDIMENT PER PERSON)

- *MUSTARDS*
- *OLIVE PASTE OR TAPENADE*
- *AIOLI*
- *HERB SPREADS*

TIMESAVER: Purchase herb dips in the deli section of the grocery store.

RARE ROAST BEEF SERVES 6 TO 12

1   3-POUND EYE OF ROUND ROAST

2   TABLESPOONS OLIVE OIL

3   TABLESPOONS CRACKED PEPPER

Here's a foolproof method for roast beef that proves it's almost as easy to roast your own rare beef as it is to buy it from a deli. Sliced right at the buffet table, a roast is a thoroughly luxurious addition to a sandwich buffet. For hosts short on time, deli roast beef is a perfectly acceptable substitution.

Preheat the oven to 325°F. Coat the roast with the olive oil and roll in the cracked pepper. Place in an oiled roasting pan and roast for about 60 minutes for rare. Transfer to a platter and let rest for at least 30 minutes before slicing, or let cool completely, cover, and refrigerate for up to 24 hours before slicing.

TIMESAVER: Purchase roast beef from a gourmet market or deli.

ROAST TURKEY BREAST SERVES 6 TO 12

1   3-POUND TURKEY BREAST

4   TABLESPOONS UNSALTED BUTTER, MELTED

3   TABLESPOONS POULTRY SEASONING

If you're already roasting the beef, why not add a turkey breast? It will roast perfectly at the same temperature and for the same length of time. Buy the poultry seasoning at any supermarket.

Preheat the oven to 325°F. Brush the turkey with the melted butter and sprinkle with the seasoning mix to evenly coat. Place in a roasting pan and roast for about 60 minutes. Transfer to a platter and let rest for 30 minutes before slicing, or let cool completely, cover, and refrigerate for up to 1 day before slicing.

TIMESAVER: Purchase roast turkey from your local grocer or deli.

OVEN-DRIED TOMATOES SERVES 8 TO 12

15 *ROMA TOMATOES, HALVED LENGTHWISE*

3   *TABLESPOONS OLIVE OIL*

2   *TABLESPOONS MIXED CHOPPED FRESH*
    OREGANO, BASIL, AND ROSEMARY, OR
    2 TEASPOONS DRIED ITALIAN HERB BLEND

These tomatoes are bursting with intense color and flavor, and are perfectly delicious in salads, on sandwiches, or chopped and added to soup.

Preheat the oven to 250°F. Place the tomatoes, cut-side up, on a baking sheet. Brush the cut sides with the olive oil and sprinkle with the herbs. Roast for 2 hours, or until shriveled but still moist. Let cool. Use now, or cover and refrigerate for up to 3 days. Return to oven temperature before serving.

TIMESAVER: Purchase oil-packed sun-dried tomatoes.

PAN-ROASTED ONIONS SERVES 8 TO 12

2   *TABLESPOONS OLIVE OIL*

3   *YELLOW ONIONS, THINLY SLICED*

2   *TABLESPOONS BALSAMIC VINEGAR*

This condiment can be made in only a few minutes and is really no more than a quick sauté. The high heat of the skillet softens onions, mellowing and enhancing their flavor. Experiment with a variety of different onions.

In a large skillet, heat the oil over medium-high heat, then add the onions and stir to coat. Sauté the onions, stirring frequently for 2 minutes or until slightly soft. Add the balsamic vinegar and toss again. Cook, stirring, for 2 minutes, then turn out on a plate to cool.

TIMESAVER: Skip the roasting and serve sliced onions.

ARUGULA-JALAPEÑO MAYONNAISE SERVES 6

2   CUPS PACKED ARUGULA

2-3 JALAPEÑO CHILIES, SEEDED AND COARSELY CHOPPED

1   CUP MAYONNAISE

This peppery spread spices up a roast beef sandwich, and is equally great as a dip for Sweet Potato Oven Fries (page 126). Add jalapeños depending on your guests' heat tolerance.

In a food processor, combine all the ingredients and process until completely smooth, about 2 minutes. Cover and refrigerate for at least 1 day or up to 3 days.

TIMESAVER: Serve a good-quality store-bought mayonnaise.

ROASTED-GARLIC SPREAD SERVES 6

3   *HEADS FRESH GARLIC*

3   *TABLESPOONS PLUS ¼ CUP OLIVE OIL*

3   *SPRIGS EACH THYME, SAGE, AND ROSEMARY*

Use this spread in place of mayonnaise or mustard or even in addition to them. If you're making the Roasted Tomato-Garlic Soup (page 127), roast the garlic for the soup alongside the garlic for this spread. If you don't have a food processor, simply mash the garlic with a fork.

To roast the garlic: Preheat the oven to 350°F. Cut 3 squares of aluminum foil slightly larger than the garlic heads. Cut a slice from the papery tip of each garlic head, exposing all the cloves. Place each garlic head on a foil square; drizzle each with 1 tablespoon olive oil and arrange 1 sprig of each herb around each head. Wrap the foil to form packets and place them on a baking sheet. Bake for 45 minutes, or until lightly browned and fragrant.

When cool, squeeze the roasted garlic cloves from their skins, and put them in a food processor. Strip the leaves from the roasted herb sprigs into the processor. With the machine running, gradually add the 1/4 cup olive oil to make an emulsified sauce.

TIMESAVER: Purchase garlic spread from a grocery store or gourmet shop.

SWEET POTATO OVEN FRIES

4   *SWEET POTATOES, PEELED AND CUT INTO*
    1/2-INCH LENGTHWISE STRIPS

3   *TABLESPOONS OLIVE OIL*

2   *TEASPOONS KOSHER SALT*

1   *TEASPOON CRACKED PEPPER*

Here's a healthier, more flavorful version of French fries. Pop these in the oven just before your guests arrive, then watch them disappear when you serve them piping hot with Arugula-Jalapeño Mayonnaise (page 123).

Line a baking sheet with parchment paper. Preheat the oven to 450°F. Put the potato strips in a large bowl. Drizzle the olive oil over and toss to coat lightly. Sprinkle with the salt and pepper and toss again. Place the potatoes in a single layer on the prepared baking sheet and bake for 15 minutes. Turn with a spatula and bake for another 15 minutes, or until golden brown.

TIMESAVER: Substitute sweet potato chips.

ROASTED TOMATO-GARLIC SOUP _{SERVES 6}

3   *POUNDS CHERRY TOMATOES, HULLED*

3   *TABLESPOONS OLIVE OIL*

3   *TABLESPOONS MINCED FRESH BASIL, MARJORAM,*
    OR OREGANO, OR A COMBINATION

6   *CLOVES ROASTED GARLIC {SEE PAGE 124}*

6   *CUPS VEGETABLE STOCK OR CANNED LOW-SALT*
    VEGETABLE BROTH

    SALT AND FRESHLY GROUND PEPPER TO TASTE

1   *TEASPOON SUGAR*

This fast soup is a fresh twist on a childhood favorite. It can be made with any ripe tomatoes, but we like the flavor and sweetness of the cherry tomatoes. Top each serving with diced Oven-Dried Tomatoes (page 121), croutons, or cheese, if you like.

Preheat the oven to 450°F. Line a jellyroll pan with parchment paper. In a large bowl, toss the tomatoes with the olive oil and herbs. Place in the prepared pan and roast for about 20 minutes, or until soft and slightly blackened. Remove from the oven and put in a food processor with the garlic cloves. Process for 1 minute, or until almost smooth. Pour the tomato mixture and stock or broth into a large pot and simmer over low heat for 20 minutes. Season with salt and pepper. Stir in the sugar.

TIMESAVER: Purchase freshly made tomato soup from a deli and reheat just before the party.

SOUP CONDIMENTS Here are just a few suggestions for soup condiments. Serve the condiments in small bowls with spoons, and invite guests to flavor their own soup to taste.

- *PARMESAN CHEESE, SLICED OR GRATED*
- *CROUTONS, STORE-BOUGHT OR FRESHLY*
  TOASTED IN THE OVEN
- *GREEN ONIONS OR CHIVES, CHOPPED*
- *FRESH HERBS, CHOPPED*

- *CRÈME FRAÎCHE*
- *SEA SALT*
- *CRACKED PEPPER*
- *BLUE CHEESE, CRUMBLED*

ONION-FENNEL SOUP SERVES 6

2   TABLESPOONS OLIVE OIL

2   LARGE OR 3 MEDIUM YELLOW ONIONS, CUT IN 1/8-INCH-THICK SLICES

2   FENNEL BULBS, TRIMMED AND SLICED CROSSWISE IN 1/8-INCH-THICK SLICES

2   TABLESPOONS MINCED FRESH THYME

6   CUPS BEEF STOCK OR CANNED LOW-SALT BEEF BROTH

SALT AND FRESHLY GROUND PEPPER TO TASTE

This soup is comforting and easy. Reserve the feathery greens from the tops of the fennel bulbs to mince for a flavorful and pretty garnish. Or, top each serving with a slice of toasted bread and a few thin slices of Gruyère cheese for a classic presentation.

In an 8-cup pot, heat the olive oil over medium heat and sauté the onions until golden, about 10 minutes. Add the fennel and cook until tender, 8 to 10 minutes. Add the thyme and sauté a few minutes more. Stir in the stock or broth. Bring to a boil, reduce the heat to a simmer, cover, and cook for 30 minutes. Season with salt and pepper.

TIMESAVER: Purchase freshly made onion soup from the deli section of the supermarket, or a premium-brand canned one, and reheat just before the party.

FLORENTINE SANDWICH COOKIES

MAKES ABOUT 3 DOZEN SANDWICH COOKIES

1/2 CUP {1 STICK} UNSALTED BUTTER, AT ROOM TEMPERATURE

1/4 CUP HEAVY CREAM

1 1/2 CUPS UNBLANCHED ALMONDS, GROUND

2 TABLESPOONS FLOUR

1 CUP SUGAR

8 OUNCES SEMISWEET CHOCOLATE, CHOPPED

These almond-infused cookies are heavenly by themselves, but even better when used to make a melted chocolate sandwich.

Preheat the oven to 375°F. Line 2 baking sheets with parchment paper.

In a medium saucepan, combine the butter and cream. Heat over medium heat until the butter has melted. Stir in the almonds, flour, and sugar. Cook until bubbly, 2 to 3 minutes. Remove from the heat.

Scoop up 1/2 teaspoonfuls of the warm batter and use a second teaspoon to scoop out rounds of batter 1 1/2 inches apart on the prepared pans. Bake in the center of the oven until lightly browned, about 6 minutes, turning the pans back to front halfway through cooking to ensure even browning. Remove from the oven and slide the parchment paper with the cookies onto a flat surface to cool completely.

In a double boiler over barely simmering water, melt the chocolate. Place 1/2 teaspoon onto a cooled cookie and gently press together with a second cookie, creating a sandwich. Continue until all the cookies are used.

TIMESAVER: Purchase cookies from a bakery or supermarket.

macaroons | lemon-poppy bundt cake | simple chocolate cake | fruit tarts | toasted-pecan clusters | assortment of cookies and candies | coffee bar | sparkling water

A DESSERT BUFFET

ON THE MENU

There is nothing more luxurious than a selection of sweets, and a dessert and coffee buffet makes any occasion special. Since the menu is not a meal, it's the perfect choice for those in-between times: late morning, afternoon, and late evening, before or after an event. Scale it down for an intimate afternoon or late evening with a few people, or make it a large gathering with all your friends. Add some festive decorations for a holiday party, move it to the kitchen for a house-warming party, center the menu around a cake for a birthday party, or create a small tray of goodies on a coffee table for an impromptu get-together with out-of-town friends.

Creating a menu entirely of desserts is an easy and practical entertaining solution, and the occasion you are celebrating will help guide your choices. Whether you choose to purchase everything from a nearby bakery, incorporate favorite family recipes, or a little of both, it's easy to customize the menu to your liking. Try to include seasonal favorites. In summer, add a cherry tart or pie and set out a bowl of fresh summer fruit such as peaches, strawberries, or berries, with a bowl of whipped cream. In the fall, substitute apples or pears in a tart or pie and serve fresh figs with ricotta cheese drizzled with honey.

Once you've decided on one or two main desserts, concentrate on some of the smaller treats to round out the buffet. You can buy or make lots of beautiful little cookies and candies, and arrange them on a tiered stand, platter, or tray. With minimal effort, a mixture of colors and textures is a simple way to enhance a table.

The coffee bar is another opportunity to allow guests to customize their preferences and experiment with new choices. A basic coffee bar should include carafes or pots of freshly brewed coffee (regular and decaf, in the best quality you can afford), cream and/or low-fat milk, and sugar. By adding a few special ingredients like flavored syrups, raw sugar, honey, ground cinnamon, unsweetened cocoa powder, and whipped cream, in addition to another type of coffee, you can create a more elaborate buffet. The ultimate coffee bar would have at least two different types of coffees plus espresso, and all of the above condiments plus lemon zest, fancy sugar cubes, foamed milk, chocolate swizzle sticks, and vanilla beans.

In addition to coffee, you may want to include some cold drinks as well. Bottles of sparkling water, flavored seltzers, juices, and a pitcher of ice-cold milk are all good choices. Keep everything cold in a big bucket filled with ice placed on a counter or on the floor near the coffee bar.

PLAN-AHEAD PARTY

TWO DAYS AHEAD	ONE DAY AHEAD	DAY OF THE PARTY	JUST BEFORE THE PARTY	DURING THE PARTY
• Decide on menu, review recipes and timesavers, and make shopping lists • Shop for groceries • Gather serving pieces, plates, linens, napkins, tableware, etc.; purchase any missing items	• Arrange furniture and set up buffet table with table-ware, serving pieces, flatware, etc. • Bake chocolate and lemon-poppy cakes; wrap tightly and store at room temperature • Make the fruit tart	• Bake chocolate pecan clusters and macaroons • Set up the coffee bar and place condiments in small containers and arrange on tray • Chill drinks in ice bucket or refrigerator • Assemble the cookie display with store-bought goodies • Ice chocolate cake and glaze lemon-poppy cake; set out on buffet	• Make a fresh pot of coffee, transfer to carafe, if using; set out containers of milk, cream, and whipped cream • Arrange the rest of the desserts on the buffet	• Restock empty platters and condiments • Refill ice bucket with drinks • Make extra pots of coffee and espresso; refill milk, cream, and whipped cream containers • Clear plates, remove empty bottles, and tidy up buffet table

SERVING IT UP

Many spaces can be used for a dessert buffet. The amount of food, number of guests, and kind of mood you want to create will help determine what you will need and where to set it up. Areas in your home that will work include a kitchen counter; a side, coffee, or console table; or a dining or patio table. Cover a folding or worktable with a floor-length cloth. If you don't have one, borrow, rent, or make one by placing a sheet of plywood on two smaller folding tables.

Creating an extraordinary buffet is easy—simply gather your serving pieces and arrange the desserts on them to make a beautiful display. Cake platters, pedestal plates, flat platters, and trays are all wonderful for serving both large and small desserts. You can make a tiered stand by stacking two or three pedestal plates on top of each other and group cookies and treats of different colors and textures side by side. Buy inexpensive round or square cake boards at a bakery supply or party store and use them for serving cakes, tarts, and condiments

from the coffee bar. Trays work equally well to contain a number of items; line them with extra napkins or pieces of cloth to add softness and texture. Paper baking cups are available in many sizes and are a great way to serve individual portions, especially of sticky or messy foods like pastry and baklava.

Aside from the serving pieces, a stack of small plates and/or bowls (depending on the kind of desserts you are serving) should be grouped at the beginning of the buffet. Napkins, forks, and/or spoons can be simply stacked, or flatware can be rolled up in the napkin, and tied with a piece of ribbon or cording.

For the coffee bar, group an espresso and/or coffeemaker, small pitchers or creamers, little bowls and plates, and plenty of cups and teaspoons. An extra coffeemaker will make things run more smoothly, and an insulated carafe or two will help keep coffee hot and fresh. Gather lots of small containers for the condiments—everything from ramekins to bread plates, small bowls, tin cups, paper candy cups, or muffin cups. Group the coffee condiments together on a tray or platter to create a beautiful and organized display. Keep things running smoothly at the coffee bar by replenishing condiments and brewing coffee, or appoint a friend or two to keep an eye on things.

INSTANT PARTY

THE NIGHT BEFORE

- Decide on menu, review recipes and timesavers, make shopping lists
- Shop for groceries, baked goods, desserts, cookies, etc.
- Gather serving pieces, plates, linens, napkins, tableware, and so on; purchase any missing items

DAY OF THE PARTY

- Arrange furniture and set up buffet
- Chill drinks in bucket or refrigerator
- If baking, set aside some time for one or two quick recipes

JUST BEFORE THE PARTY

- Make a fresh pot of coffee, transfer to carafe, if using; set out containers of milk, cream, and whipped cream
- Arrange the desserts on the buffet
- Assemble cookie display with store-bought goodies

DURING THE PARTY

- Restock empty platters and condiments
- Refill ice bucket with drinks
- Make extra pots of coffee and espresso; refill milk, cream, and whipped cream containers
- Clear plates, remove empty bottles, and tidy up buffet table

MACAROONS MAKES 25 TO 30 COOKIES

2   EGG WHITES

1/2   TEASPOON VANILLA EXTRACT

2/3   CUP SUGAR

1 1/3   CUPS FLAKED COCONUT

Light as air, these classic cookies benefit from the addition of 1/2 cup chopped almonds, pecans, or hazelnuts in the batter.

Preheat the oven to 325°F. Line 2 baking sheets with parchment paper.

In a large bowl, beat the egg whites with the vanilla until soft peaks form. Gradually beat in the sugar until stiff, glossy peaks form. Gently fold in the coconut flakes. Drop generous teaspoonfuls of batter 2 inches apart onto the prepared pans. Bake for 20 minutes, or until the edges are lightly browned. Transfer the macaroons to a wire rack and let cool completely.

TIMESAVER: Purchase plain or chocolate-dipped macaroons from a bakery.

LEMON-POPPY BUNDT CAKE SERVES 6 TO 8

1   BOX LEMON CAKE MIX

1¹/₂ CUPS WATER

¹/₂   CUP CANOLA OIL

2   TABLESPOONS POPPY SEEDS

3   EGGS

Crunchy poppy seeds add interest to a simple lemon box-mix cake. Lemon-lovers can add 2 tablespoons grated lemon zest to the batter for extra zing.

Preheat the oven to 350°F. Lightly spray a 10-inch bundt pan with vegetable-oil cooking spray. Put the cake mix in a large bowl. Add the remaining ingredients and beat with an electric mixer on low speed for 1 minute or beat 2 minutes by hand. Pour into the prepared pan. Bake 35 to 40 minutes, or until a toothpick inserted in the center comes out clean. Allow the cake to cool completely before removing from the pan.

TIMESAVER: Purchase a lemon-poppy seed cake from a bakery, or substitute pound cake, lemon meringue pie, or coffee cake.

LEMON FROSTING MAKES 1/2 CUP, ENOUGH FOR 1 BUNDT CAKE

1   CUP CONFECTIONERS' SUGAR

¹/₄   CUP FRESH LEMON JUICE

1   TABLESPOON GRATED LEMON ZEST

This frosting couldn't be simpler, and looks beautiful drizzled over a bundt cake.

In a large bowl, combine the sugar and lemon juice; stir to blend. Drizzle the frosting over the top of the cake and allow it to drip over the sides. Sprinkle the lemon zest over the top of the cake.

TIMESAVER: Sprinkle the cake with powered sugar rather than frosting it.

SIMPLE CHOCOLATE CAKE SERVES 6 TO 8

1   BOX CHOCOLATE CAKE MIX

1½ CUPS WATER

½ CUP CANOLA OIL

3   EGGS

½ CUP SEMISWEET CHOCOLATE CHIPS

CHOCOLATE FROSTING {RECIPE FOLLOWS}

This easy chocolate cake is prepared from a box mix and enriched with the addition of chocolate chips.

Preheat the oven to 350°F. Lightly spray two 8-inch round baking pans with vegetable-oil cooking spray. Put the cake mix in a large bowl and add the water, oil, and eggs. Beat on low speed for 1 minute or stir for 2 minutes by hand, or until smooth. Do not overmix. Gently fold in the chocolate chips. Pour into the prepared pans and bake for 30 to 35 minutes, or until a toothpick inserted in the center comes out clean. Leave in the pans to let cool completely before removing.

TIMESAVER: Purchase chocolate cake from a bakery or garnish it simply with a sprinkling of powdered sugar, fresh berries, and warmed hot fudge sauce.

CHOCOLATE FROSTING MAKES 2 CUPS, ENOUGH FOR TWO 8- OR 9-INCH CAKE LAYERS

4¾ CUPS SIFTED CONFECTIONERS' SUGAR

½ CUP UNSWEETENED COCOA POWDER

½ CUP {1 STICK} UNSALTED BUTTER,
   AT ROOM TEMPERATURE

⅓ CUP BOILING WATER

1   TEASPOON VANILLA EXTRACT

Prepare this creamy frosting ahead of time and refrigerate for up to 3 hours.

In a large bowl, stir the sugar and cocoa powder together. Add the butter, then stir in the boiling water and vanilla. Beat with an electric mixer on low speed until smooth; increase speed to medium and beat for 1 minute. Let cool for 20 to 30 minutes, or until spreadable. Frost the top of one cake layer. Top with remaining cake layer and frost the sides and top smoothly and evenly.

TIMESAVER: Purchase prepared frosting in baking section of a grocery store.

FRUIT TARTS MAKES 24 MINI TARTS

1/2 CUP CHOPPED PISTACHIO NUTS

2 CUPS CHOCOLATE OR VANILLA PUDDING

24 PREMADE MINI TART SHELLS {FOUND IN SPECIALTY FOOD STORES AND BAKERIES}

4 PINTS FRESH BERRIES, SUCH AS BLUEBERRIES, BLACKBERRIES, OR RASPBERRIES

24 FRESH MINT LEAVES

Mini fruit tarts are the quintessential summer dessert. Select according to the season. Fresh berries are a simple and delicious choice, but seasonal fruits such as sliced peaches, kiwis, and nectarines work equally well.

Stir the pistachio nuts into the pudding . Spoon a heaping tablespoon of the pudding mixture into the tart shells and top with berries. Top each tart with a mint leaf. Refrigerate for up to 6 hours before serving.

TIMESAVER: Purchase fruit tarts or fruit pie from a bakery.

TOASTED-PECAN CLUSTERS MAKES 14 TO 18 CLUSTERS

2 POUNDS PECAN HALVES

2 POUNDS MILK CHOCOLATE, CHOPPED

Use a good quality milk chocolate to make these decadent sweets. Substitute your favorite nut, or try a combination of a few varieties.

Line a baking sheet with parchment paper. In a dry skillet over medium heat, toast the nuts for 2 to 3 minutes, or until fragrant. Pour into a sieve and let cool for 5 minutes. In a double boiler over barely simmering water, melt the chocolate. Put the strainer holding the nuts in a medium bowl. Pour the warm chocolate over the nuts. Mound tablespoonfuls of chocolate-covered nuts on the prepared pan. Let cool until set, about 30 minutes.

TIMESAVER: Visit your local chocolatier for an assortment of tasty confections, or make walnut brownies from a mix.

A true crowd pleaser, the cocktail and hors d'oeuvre party is the ultimate in entertaining. And for good reason: Cocktail parties are easy to plan and prepare, work well in almost all spaces, and are a great way to bring people together from all walks of life. With the right combination of food, drink, lighting, and music, you can create a night to remember.

COCKTAILS &
HORS D'OEUVRES

Whether you're planning a cocktail party to celebrate a birthday, holiday, anniversary, promotion, or just for fun, a good place to start is with your budget. How much you want to spend will determine the number of guests you can invite, what you can serve, and how lavishly you can decorate. As always, we recommend simplicity. If you serve a few choice drinks, a small but delectable array of food, and decorate stylishly but modestly, you'll be amazed by how many people you can entertain with a limited amount of money.

With your budget in mind, continue your planning by selecting a theme for your party. A Christmas holiday party with seasonal colors and decor, a Hawaiian luau replete with tropical fruits and exotic flowers, a refined evening of wine and cheeses—these are all great themes. But don't limit yourself to tradition—how about a martini party; an evening of sake, sushi, and Japanese beers; or a night of frozen drinks and spicy foods? You could even choose a color as your theme, say red, and create a selection of cocktails in hues of red and a menu with equal chromatic appeal.

Once you decide on your theme, you'll have a pretty good idea of what cocktails you should be serving. Try to limit your selection to one or two cocktails, plus wine, beer, soft drinks, and water. Not only will this make your life easier, it will bring focus to your party and leave a lasting impression with your guests.

Unlike a sit-down dinner or buffet, where the beverage is chosen to complement the meal, the cocktail party works in reverse. Choose your drinks, then choose hors d'oeuvres that complement your selection. And, of course, keeping your selection simple applies to the menu just as well as the drinks. If you're having an outdoor summer cocktail party, try grilled chicken and vegetable skewers, with a selection of dipping sauces. Just remember that ease of serving and consuming is essential at cocktail parties. Since most guests remain standing, choose finger foods or bites you can serve with food picks. To cut your workload, choose foods that can be served at room temperature or chilled. And as with all parties, feel free to mix store-bought dishes with homemade ones and include foods that can be made in advance. Finally, remember that hors d'oeuvres are a great way to get people to try new flavors and foods. Some people shy away from adventurous eating when it comes to a full entrée, but most will try a tantalizing morsel.

When it comes time to set up the bar for your cocktail party, there are a few things to remember. Whether you're having a small get-together or a large group, you'll need to stock the bar with a cocktail shaker, a corkscrew, a bottle opener, napkins, stirrers, ice, and water. Most of these things you'll have on hand, but if you're short on glasses it's easy to borrow from friends, or even rent from party suppliers. Clear plastic tumblers work in a pinch; they look great adorned with a paper umbrella or colorful cocktail stirrer, and clean-up is a breeze. You'll also need to supply the spirits and garnishes, but what kind and how much will depend on what cocktails you're serving. Another must these days is a selection of nonalcoholic beverages. Beyond soft drinks and water, consider creating a nonalcoholic version of one or two cocktails for guests who do not drink or for those who are driving.

For a small party, a self-service bar is easy and inexpensive. To set up a self-service bar, simply stack up a few rows of glasses, lay out napkins, ice, garnishes, and bar tools, and have a trash can nearby. If you've selected a special cocktail or two, prepare the drinks ahead of time in pitchers and set them out for the guests to pour themselves. If you're also serving beer and wine, put the bottles in ice and set them on your bar. Check the bar frequently during the party, restocking the beverages and ice throughout the evening. For large groups of 12 or more, consider hiring a bartender. It's an added expense, but for that special occasion, the help of a bartender leaves you free to mingle with your guests.

When it comes to serving hors d'oeuvres, you have two choices: buffet or tray service. The buffet is, of course, the less expensive and more common route. But inexpensive doesn't mean it can't be elegant. Creating an hors d'oeuvre buffet is an opportunity to bring color and style to your party. Be sure to include plates, napkins, and cocktail picks. For additional buffet tips and ideas, see the Buffets chapter. Or, you can go the tray-service route. In this case, hired help will be responsible for serving your guests the hors d'oeuvres and picking up the used plates, napkins, and glasses.

There are as many ways to set up and decorate your cocktail party as there are themes. Start by creating the bar and buffet table and work your way around the room. You can transform just about any table or surface into a focal point with the simple addition of table linens, fabrics, or woven runners. You can also spruce up surfaces with flower petals, tropical leaves, floating flowers, or votive candles.

How you choose to light the room is important for all occasions, but particularly for cocktail parties. Since most cocktail parties take place in the evening or at night, you'll have the opportunity to control the lighting of your space to create a specific mood or ambience. If your party is indoors, try grouping candles in important places, like around the bar or on the buffet. Hanging lanterns are another great way to light an indoor space, as are strings of decorative lights, or create colorful backdrops by placing lights behind panels of fabric strung from the ceiling. If nothing else, you can at least dim the house lights. For outdoor parties, tiki torches create a dramatic effect, as do hanging lanterns in trees, floating candles in pools, or groups of candles in areas where you want people to congregate.

The last element for successful cocktail parties is great music. Naturally, you'll want to pick music that fits with the theme of your party and that adds to the mood you're creating. Be sure to keep it at a volume where people can enjoy it and still converse easily with one another.

In this chapter, we've pulled all the elements of successful cocktail parties together with two completely different themes. First up, an outdoor Indian Cocktail Party in a festive palette of hot pink and orange. And second, an indoor Holiday Wine & Cheese Party, with a new approach to holiday colors and decor.

carrot-ginger soup | lamb chops with cucumber-yogurt dip | roasted-eggplant dip with naan chips | saffron-ginger rice cakes with spicy shrimp | spicy nuts | mango crunch | ginger-lime gimlets | dates | middle eastern teas

INDIAN COCKTAIL PARTY

ON THE MENU

This distinctive cocktail party is the perfect backdrop for festive occasions such as celebrating a promotion, a birthday, a holiday, a graduation, or even a coed wedding shower, anniversary, or engagement party. From an intimate gathering with a few friends to a bash for thirty, the Indian Cocktail Party is exotic, versatile, and memorable.

The menu and recipes are designed to keep preparation and fuss at a minimum. Dips and drink mixes are the easiest to make ahead, and hors d'oeuvres can be cooked in batches so you don't have to slave in the kitchen for hours. Prepare them ahead of time so you can enjoy the party as much as your guests, or pick up an assortment of items from a local Indian restaurant if you're short on time. Ethnic grocers, world markets, and gourmet shops are an excellent source for prepared foods, ingredients, and inexpensive tableware and decorations.

Start the party off with a cocktail created especially for it. A batch of Ginger-Lime Gimlets is easy to make ahead. Serve them from a pitcher or have a friend play bartender and mix up a few at a time. Aside from a special cocktail, you have many choices when it comes to drinks. To simplify and cut costs, round out the cocktails with wine, Indian beer, and flavored seltzers.

Indian foods offer a rich variety of flavors and textures. Broil a big batch of lamb chops just before the party and serve them with a cool cucumber dipping sauce. Roasted eggplant and Indian spices can be transformed into a creamy dip for crunchy naan chips. Carrot-ginger soup is especially easy to make for a large group. Serve it hot or cold, and treat your guests to tiny tastes. Ladle small portions of the flavorful soup into cups for sipping; sake cups, condiment bowls, or even cordial glasses work well. Basmati cakes with spicy shrimp look fancy but are easy to make. The cakes can be made in advance, or wedges of Indian bread or rice crackers can be substituted. India is famous for its sweets, so carry on the tradition and offer a tray of goodies from an Indian market or make them yourself. Dates, coconut cakes, pistachio bars, and sweet nuts are just a few examples, and they all look beautiful when arranged on a tray or platter.

PLAN-AHEAD PARTY

TWO DAYS AHEAD	ONE DAY AHEAD	DAY OF THE PARTY	JUST BEFORE THE PARTY	DURING THE PARTY
• Decide on menu, review recipes and timesavers, and make shopping lists • Shop for groceries • Gather serving pieces, plates, linens, napkins, tableware, and so on; purchase any missing items • Make drink mixes	• Make the soup and roasted eggplant dip; refrigerate • Make the rice cakes and spicy shrimp • Make Spicy Nuts and Cucumber-Yogurt Dip • Marinate lamb chops • Make Mango Crunch	• Arrange furniture and set up bar and hors d'oeuvre tables with plates, barware, serving pieces, decorations, lighting, and so on • Stock bar with garnishes, cocktail picks, and napkins • Chill drinks in an ice bucket or the refrigerator • Arrange hors d'oeuvres on serving pieces and transfer dips and sauces to small bowls	• Set hors d'oeuvre platters on tables; light hibachis and candles • Broil lamb chops and arrange on serving platter • Set drinks and mixes out on bar	• Restock the empty hors d'oeuvre platters and dipping sauces • Refill the drink mixes and restock the ice bucket with drinks • Clear plates, remove empty bottles, and tidy up bar and hors d'oeuvre tables • Serve Mango Crunch

SERVING IT UP

Whether out in the garden on a hot summer night or in front of the fire in the living room, your Indian Cocktail Party can be held in several areas of the home. Find two places to set up the food and cocktails. Indoors or out, a dining table, console, patio, or folding table for the hors d'oeuvres can be draped with extra fabric, tablecloths, pareos, or saris. In the garden, take advantage of any outdoor structures such as pergolas or overhead trellises by draping them with inexpensive fabric to make an instant canopy over your hors d'oeuvre and drink tables.

The bar table needs to be very accessible to keep things running smoothly during the party. Keep the area around the bar table as open as possible, so that guests can approach it from a few different directions. Spend some time organizing the bar and stocking it with everything your guests will need. A pitcher of Ginger-Lime Gimlets should have a special place, along with a tray of glasses, napkins, and garnishes to make serving easy. Red wine can be lined up on another area of the table, with chilled wine, beer, and seltzers in an ice bucket nearby. Place glasses on the table in a neat row along with a stack of cocktail napkins, a corkscrew, and any garnishes or condiments.

Use the rich and vibrant colors of India in your color palette. All you need are some colorful fabrics—oranges, pinks, and reds look wonderful together and you can mix and match patterns and prints as long as the colors work. Clean scarves, saris, pareos, extra pieces of a fabric, and tablecloths can double as tablecloths, runners, or canopies.

With a colorful backdrop and party area in place, gather items from around your house to use on the table. India is known for its metalware, so make use of stainless steel, old pewter, and tin—they will look charming when mixed with beautiful fabrics. Woven trays; wood, bamboo, and stone serving pieces are also useful and work with just about any color scheme. Float bright-colored flowers like dahlias or orchids in low bowls on the table. Provide small cups of toothpicks, a stack of napkins, and some small plates or forks so that guests can serve themselves with ease.

For an evening party, hang colorful lanterns or a few strings of tiny lights around the party area. Torches stuck in the ground and hanging lanterns give off lots of light when grouped around areas where guests will be mingling and are essential in keeping the party lively throughout the evening. On the bar, hors d'oeuvre tables, and on tables or ledges around seating areas, use floating candles, pillars, and votives to cast a warm glow.

INSTANT PARTY

THE NIGHT BEFORE	DAY OF THE PARTY	JUST BEFORE THE PARTY	DURING THE PARTY
• Decide on menu, review recipes and timesavers, and make shopping lists	• Set up bar and hors d'oeuvre tables with linens, tableware, barware, decorations, lighting, and so on	• Arrange hors d'oeuvres on serving pieces and transfer dips and sauces to small bowls	• Restock empty hors d'oeuvre platters and dipping sauces
• Shop for groceries, baked goods, and prepared foods	• Make drink mixes and chill drinks in ice bucket or refrigerator	• Set hors d'oeuvre platters on tables; light hibachis and candles	• Refill drink mixes and restock ice bucket with drinks
• Gather serving pieces, plates, napkins, tableware, and so on; purchase any missing items	• Make Spicy Shrimp and refrigerate	• Broil lamb chops and arrange on serving platter	• Clear plates, remove empty bottles, and tidy up bar and hors d'oeuvre tables
		• Set drinks and mixes out on bar	• Serve sorbet and candied ginger
		• Season and reheat carrot soup	

CARROT-GINGER SOUP ^{SERVES 6 TO 8}

2   TABLESPOONS OLIVE OIL

1   YELLOW ONION, FINELY CHOPPED

1½ POUNDS CARROTS, PEELED AND
     FINELY CHOPPED

2   TABLESPOONS PEELED, MINCED
     FRESH GINGER

1   TABLESPOON GROUND CUMIN

1   TEASPOON SALT

1   TEASPOON CAYENNE PEPPER

6   CUPS VEGETABLE STOCK OR CANNED
     LOW-SALT VEGETABLE BROTH

Serve this delicious soup steaming hot on a chilly night or ice cold on a hot summer evening. Garnish it with thin strips of candied ginger or a dollop of plain yogurt.

In a large pot, heat the olive oil over medium-high heat, add the onion, and sauté until soft, about 5 minutes. Add the carrots, ginger, cumin, salt, and cayenne and cook for 5 minutes, stirring occasionally. Add the stock or broth and bring to a boil, then reduce heat and simmer until the vegetables are tender, about 20 minutes. In a blender or food processor, puree the soup in batches until smooth. If serving hot, return the soup to the pan and rewarm over low heat. To make ahead, let cool, cover, and refrigerate for up to 2 days. To serve cold, let cool, cover, and refrigerate for at least 1 hour.

TIMESAVER: Buy carrot soup from a gourmet grocery store or buy a good-quality canned carrot soup; add seasonings to taste.

LAMB CHOPS WITH CUCUMBER-YOGURT DIP SERVES 6

CUCUMBER-YOGURT DIP

1 CUP PLAIN YOGURT

1/2 CUCUMBER, PEELED, SEEDED, AND FINELY CHOPPED

2 TABLESPOONS FINELY CHOPPED RED ONION

1 TABLESPOON FRESH LEMON JUICE

GRATED ZEST OF 1 LEMON

MARINADE

GRATED ZEST OF 2 LEMONS

1/4 CUP FRESH LEMON JUICE

6 CLOVES GARLIC, MINCED

2 TABLESPOONS MINCED FRESH ROSEMARY

1 TABLESPOON GARAM MASALA

2 TEASPOONS KOSHER SALT

1 TEASPOON CRACKED PEPPER

1/2 CUP OLIVE OIL

12-14 LAMB CHOPS, TRIMMED TO APPROXIMATELY 1/2 INCH THICK AND FRENCHED

Garam masala is a mixture of Indian spices; you can find it already mixed in specialty shops and some well-stocked supermarkets. Ask your butcher to cut the lamb for you, keeping the bones as long as possible and Frenching them. Plan on 2 chops per person.

To make the dip: In a small bowl, combine all the dip ingredients and mix well. Cover and refrigerate for at least 1 hour or up to 24 hours.

To make the marinade: In a small bowl, combine the lemon zest and juice, garlic, rosemary, garam masala, salt, and pepper. Gradually whisk in the olive oil until well blended.

Put the lamb chops in a bowl, add the marinade, and toss to coat. Cover and let sit at room temperature for 1 hour, or refrigerate for up to 24 hours.

If refrigerated, remove the lamb chops from the refrigerator 30 minutes before broiling. Preheat the broiler. Remove the chops from the marinade and broil about 5 inches from the heat source for 5 minutes on each side for medium-rare. Check for preferred doneness.

TIMESAVER: Buy a prepared cucumber-yogurt dip from the grocery store or an Indian restaurant.

CHAPTER FIVE: COCKTAILS & HORS D'OEUVRES

ROASTED-EGGPLANT DIP
WITH NAAN CHIPS ^{SERVES 6}

ROASTED-EGGPLANT DIP

1   *LARGE EGGPLANT, HALVED LENGTHWISE*

2   *TABLESPOONS OLIVE OIL, PLUS MORE FOR BRUSHING AND DRIZZLING*

1   *HEAD ROASTED GARLIC (SEE PAGE 124)*

2   *TABLESPOONS FRESH LEMON JUICE*

1   *TEASPOON KOSHER SALT*

1   *TEASPOON GARAM MASALA*

1/2   *TEASPOON CRACKED PEPPER*

NAAN CHIPS

2   *OVALS NAAN BREAD, ABOUT 12 INCHES LONG*

    OLIVE OIL FOR BRUSHING

Eggplant is transformed by roasting, becoming velvety smooth and luxurious in texture. This simple dip is delicious with the naan chips, but it goes equally well with triangles of plain naan, pita bread, or crunchy pappadams.

To make the dip: Preheat the oven to 425°F. Line a baking sheet with aluminum foil. Brush the cut sides of the eggplant with olive oil and place, cut-side down, on the prepared pan. Roast for about 35 minutes, or until soft. Remove from the oven and let cool. Scrape the eggplant flesh from the skin into a food processor. Add the roasted garlic cloves, the 2 tablespoons olive oil, the lemon juice, salt, garam masala, and pepper. Process for 1 minute or until smooth. Cover and refrigerate for at least 1 hour or up to 24 hours. To serve, spoon into a small bowl and drizzle with olive oil.

To make the chips: Preheat the oven to 350°F. Line a large baking sheet with parchment paper. Cut each naan into chip-size pieces, about 2 by 3 inches. Brush the top of each piece lightly with olive oil. Place in a single layer on the prepared pan. Bake for 10 to 15 minutes, or until the chips are slightly crisp and golden brown. Remove from the oven and let cool slightly before serving. Or let cool completely, store in an airtight container for up to two days, and serve at room temperature.

TIMESAVER: Buy naan chips from a gourmet shop, Indian market, or Indian restaurant, and substitute hummus for the eggplant dip.

SAFFRON-GINGER RICE CAKES WITH SPICY SHRIMP SERVES 6

SAFFRON-GINGER RICE CAKES

1   CUP WATER

1   TEASPOON KOSHER SALT

1/2   CUP BASMATI RICE

1/4   TEASPOON THREAD SAFFRON
       (OR A SMALL PINCH)

1   TABLESPOON CANDIED GINGER,
       VERY FINELY MINCED

1   EGG WHITE, BEATEN LIGHTLY

3   TABLESPOONS OLIVE OIL

SPICY SHRIMP

18-20 MEDIUM SHRIMP, COOKED
       AND SHELLED

1   TABLESPOON OLIVE OIL

1   TABLESPOON CURRY POWDER

1/2   CUP CHUTNEY (MAJOR GREY'S IS GOOD)

       CILANTRO LEAVES FOR GARNISH

This recipe will come together very quickly if you prepare the rice cakes a day ahead and buy your shrimp cooked and shelled. Assemble the cakes just before the party.

To make the rice cakes: In a medium saucepan, bring the water to a boil and add the salt, rice, saffron, and ginger. Stir and return to a boil, then reduce heat to low, cover and cook until the rice is tender, and the water is absorbed, about 20 minutes. Remove from heat and let cool.

Put the rice in a bowl, pour the egg white over, and mix well. Form 2 tablespoons at a time into a ball, press it flat between your palms, and place on a tray. In a medium nonstick skillet, heat 1 tablespoon of the olive oil over medium-high heat and cook 5 or 6 rice cakes until golden brown, 3 to 4 minutes per side. Repeat with the remaining rice patties and oil. Serve now, or let cool, cover, and refrigerate for up to 1 day. To reheat, place on a parchment-lined baking sheet and bake in a preheated 400°F oven for 5 minutes.

To make the shrimp: Put the shrimp in a bowl. Toss with the olive oil, add the curry, and toss again to coat thoroughly. Adjust seasoning to taste. Cover and refrigerate for at least 1 hour and up to 1 day. To assemble, place 1/2 teaspoon chutney on each rice cake and top with a shrimp and a cilantro leaf.

TIMESAVER: Buy Indian crackers, or toast pita wedges and top with the shrimp.

CHAPTER FIVE: COCKTAILS & HORS D'OEUVRES

SPICY NUTS MAKES ABOUT 4 CUPS

1   *POUND UNSALTED NUTS*

1   *TABLESPOON UNSALTED BUTTER*

1   *TABLESPOON GARAM MASALA*

Nearly any kind of nuts can be used in this recipe, as long as they are unsalted. We prefer to use pistachios and cashews because they are a little more unexpected, and they complement the other flavors in this menu. Garam masala is available in most grocery stores, or you can substitute curry powder or a mild chili powder.

In a large skillet, toast the nuts over medium heat, stirring frequently, until fragrant, about 8 minutes. Watch carefully, as once they begin to brown they can burn quickly. Add the butter and continue to stir until the nuts are coated. Stir in the spice and toast a few more minutes, or until fragrant. Pour into a bowl and let cool. Use now, or store in an airtight container for up to 5 days.

TIMESAVER: Buy spiced nuts from a gourmet shop and reheat in the oven just before serving.

MANGO CRUNCH SERVES 6

2   *CUPS {8 OUNCES} PISTACHIO NUTS, PREFERABLY UNSALTED*

1   *TABLESPOON UNSALTED BUTTER*

2   *TABLESPOONS SUGAR*

¹/₄ *CUP CANDIED GINGER, MINCED*

1   *QUART MANGO SORBET*

¹/₂ *MANGO, PEELED, CUT FROM PIT, AND FINELY DICED*

Sorbet is a traditional palate cleanser, and a tiny scoop of mango sorbet hidden beneath a blanket of crunchy nuts and fresh chopped mango is sure to delight the senses. These little bites are tantalizing served in a small cup or other interesting container.

In a large skillet over medium heat, toast the nuts, stirring frequently, until fragrant, about 8 minutes. Watch carefully, as once they begin to brown they can burn quickly. Add the butter and stir to coat the nuts. Add the sugar and stir again. Add the minced ginger and cook a few more minutes, or until the sugar has adhered to the nuts. Pour onto a plate and let cool.

To serve, place a small scoop of mango sorbet in a cup and top with 1 tablespoon of nut mixture and 1 tablespoon of diced mango.

TIMESAVER: Top the sorbet with minced candied ginger.

GINGER-LIME GIMLETS

FOR EACH GIMLET:

ICE CUBES

2　*OUNCES {¹/₄ CUP} VODKA OR GIN*

2　*TABLESPOONS GINGER-INFUSED SIMPLE SYRUP {RECIPE FOLLOWS}*

2　*TABLESPOONS FRESHLY SQUEEZED LIME JUICE*

A gimlet can be made with either vodka or gin, and served straight up or on the rocks, with or without a sugar rim on the glass. To sugar the rim of a glass, run a small wedge of lime around the rim and place the glass upside down on a small plate of sugar. Shake off any extra sugar and fill. Garnish with a piece of candied ginger and a wedge of lime if desired.

Fill a cocktail mixing beaker with ice cubes, add all the remaining ingredients, and stir well. Serve on the rocks or strained.

TIMESAVER: Substitute presweetened lime juice for the simple syrup and fresh juice.

GINGER-INFUSED SIMPLE SYRUP MAKES 2 CUPS

2　*CUPS SUGAR*

2　*CUPS WATER*

1　*3-INCH PIECE FRESH GINGER, PEELED AND CUT INTO ¹/₄-INCH SLICES*

In a small saucepan, combine all the ingredients and cook over medium heat, stirring until the sugar has dissolved. Continue to cook until the mixture has thickened slightly, about 6 to 8 minutes. Do not boil. Remove from the heat and let cool. Strain to remove the ginger pieces. Store in a covered jar in the refrigerator for up to 3 days.

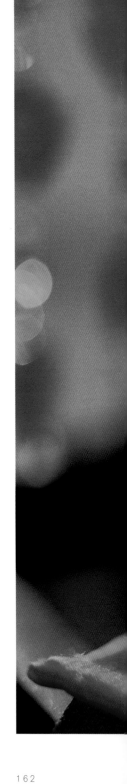

CHAPTER FIVE: COCKTAILS & HORS D'OEUVRES

holiday cheese display | selection of wines and cheeses | fondue with condiments | elegant fresh fruit | seared scallops with exotic spices | beef and mushroom skewers with red wine sauce | sensational sweet nuts | nonalcoholic glögg | breads and crackers | condiments and nibbles

HOLIDAY WINE & CHEESE PARTY

ON THE MENU

Explore the culinary world of wine and cheese with a stylish get-together with friends. An afternoon or evening discovering new tastes and traditions is a fun and easy way to entertain. Just about any occasion that calls for casual elegance is cause for this kind of celebration, whether it's a birthday, a housewarming, an anniversary, or an engagement party. Dress it up for a sophisticated holiday party, center your theme around a culinary region, or take it outdoors for an elegant picnic in the garden. It's also a great way to create an ongoing tradition in your home, varying your theme each time.

The cultures and traditions of many wine-producing regions make it easy to find a theme for your party. Popular wine-producing regions like France, Italy, Spain, and California have an abundance of wines that are readily available in most markets. There are also many smaller wine-producing regions scattered throughout the States. Some of these lesser-known spots are gaining popularity on the wine scene, and oftentimes you will find a local dairy producing quality cheeses as well. Stage a large gathering around a selection of wines and cheeses from a few different regions. Not only will it give you a general idea of what each offers, but it is also fun to compare them. A smaller party might center around one particular variety of wine—Pinot Noir,

Shiraz, or Merlot, for example—or be entirely devoted to a single region. To cut costs and involve your guests, have each one bring a bottle of wine or a cheese from the region or type you've chosen for your party.

With your theme and culinary framework in place, it's time to begin choosing the wines and cheeses for your menu. Where you start is entirely up to you, and part of the fun is learning about the range of choices available. There are many opinions about how to select wine and cheese, and you can gain a lot of information from a visit to a specialty wine, cheese, or gourmet shop in your neighborhood. Such places can provide lots of information and are willing to let you taste a few samples of the things they carry. In addition, plenty of information is available from magazines, books, and the Internet.

Wine combines easily with most foods. If you are exploring a regional theme, serve specialty foods of the region. Also consider the taste of the pairings. Beef tenderloin and mushroom skewers match well with red wine, while baked scallops are more suited to a crisp white. Of course, traditional favorites like seasonal fruits, rustic breads, and olives are always a welcome addition to any wine and cheese hors d'oeuvre table.

PLAN-AHEAD PARTY

TWO DAYS AHEAD	ONE DAY AHEAD	DAY OF THE PARTY	JUST BEFORE THE PARTY	DURING THE PARTY
• Decide on menu, review recipes and timesavers, and make shopping lists • Shop for groceries • Gather serving pieces, plates, linens, napkins, tableware, and so on; purchase any missing items	• Arrange furniture and set up tables with linens, tableware, glassware, decorations, lighting, and so on • Make Sensational Sweet Nuts and store in an airtight container • Wash and prep vegetables and cube bread for fondue	• Arrange fruit display • Chill drinks in an ice bucket or refrigerator • Arrange cheeses, breads, and crackers on serving pieces, and put dips and nibbles in small bowls • Make Beef and Mushroom Skewers • Make Fondue with Condiments • Make glögg	• Transfer fondue to pot on table • Arrange Beef and Mushroom Skewers on a platter • Set wine, drinks, and/or ice buckets on table • Reheat glögg	• Restock empty hors d'oeuvre platters and fondue pot • Bake scallops, arrange on platter, and serve immediately • Restock tables and ice buckets with wine and water • Clear plates, remove empty bottles, and tidy up tables

SERVING IT UP

Serving up wine and cheese is delightfully simple. Depending on the space available and the number of guests you've invited, there are several ways to organize your party area. Start by organizing the wines you've selected by type or region. For one large table such as a countertop or buffet, dining, or coffee table, arrange an edible fruit centerpiece in the center with some of the other hors d'oeuvres grouped nearby. Whether they are on different areas of the table or placed side by side, keep the appropriate wines, cheeses, and hors d'oeuvres together. Use the same setup if you have several smaller tables like a side table, console, or cocktail table, but make a grouping for each table of wines, cheeses, and a few hors d'oeuvres.

Most of the serving essentials you will need are things you probably own. A stack of small plates, napkins, food picks or forks, a few corkscrews, and plenty of wineglasses are essential. Place rows of wineglasses next to the bottles of wine along with a corkscrew so guests can serve themselves. A marble or wood cutting board and knives are ideal for serving breads and cheeses. A tiered pedestal platter or cake plate is perfect for creating a stylish fruit display. A fondue pot with sterno burner will keep cheese bubbling through the evening.

INSTANT PARTY

THE NIGHT BEFORE

- Decide on menu, review recipes and timesavers, and make shopping lists
- Shop for groceries
- Gather serving pieces, linens, napkins, tableware, and so on; purchase any missing items

DAY OF THE PARTY

- Arrange furniture and set up tables with linens, tableware, glassware, decorations, lighting, and so on
- Thread beef and mushrooms onto skewers
- Arrange fruit display and prep bread for fondue
- Chill drinks in an ice bucket or refrigerator
- Arrange cheeses, breads, and crackers on serving pieces, and put dips and nibbles in small bowls
- Transfer nuts to a serving bowl

JUST BEFORE THE PARTY

- Make fondue and transfer to a fondue pot on table
- Broil Beef and Mushroom Skewers and arrange on platter
- Set wine, drinks, and/or ice buckets on table
- Heat apple cider
- Roast scallops, arrange on a platter

DURING THE PARTY

- Restock empty hors d'oeuvre platters and fondue pot
- Restock tables and ice buckets with wine and water
- Clear plates, remove empty bottles, and tidy up tables

HOLIDAY CHEESE DISPLAY SERVES 6

2	TABLESPOONS MINCED FRESH THYME
1	TABLESPOON MINCED FRESH ROSEMARY
4	FRESH BASIL LEAVES, MINCED
1	LOG FRESH WHITE GOAT CHEESE
1	WEDGE BLUE CHEESE
1	WEDGE CAMEMBERT OR BRIE CHEESE
1	WEDGE SWISS CHEESE
1	WEDGE PORT SALUT CHEESE
1	POUND RED AND GREEN GRAPES
	RUSTIC BREAD AND ASSORTED CRACKERS

Herb-crusted goat cheese is an elegant addition to this selection. When fresh herbs are scarce, roll the goat cheese in cracked black pepper instead. Add personal favorites or regional cheeses to make an interesting assortment.

In a shallow bowl, combine the herbs and mix well. Roll the goat cheese in the herbs to coat completely. Arrange with the remaining cheeses and grapes on a platter as desired. Serve with breads and crackers.

TIMESAVER: Purchase herbed goat cheese from a cheese store or gourmet grocery.

SELECTION OF WINES AND CHEESES

- SPANISH RIOJA WITH MANCHEGO CHEESE
- FRENCH BORDEAUX WITH ROQUEFORT
- CALIFORNIA CHARDONNAY WITH BRIE, CAMEMBERT, OR PORT SALUT
- OREGON PINOT NOIR WITH GOAT CHEESE OR SHARP CHEDDAR

CHAPTER FIVE: COCKTAILS & HORS D'OEUVRES

FONDUE WITH CONDIMENTS SERVES 6

1   POUND FINGERLING POTATOES, HALVED

2   TABLESPOONS OLIVE OIL

1   TABLESPOON SEA SALT

2   GREEN APPLES, CORED AND CUT INTO WEDGES

2   TEASPOONS FRESH LEMON JUICE

1   POUND ASPARAGUS, BLANCHED FOR 3 TO 5 MINUTES

1   BUNCH BROCCOLI, CUT INTO FLORETS AND BLANCHED FOR 3 TO 5 MINUTES

1   LOAF RUSTIC BREAD, CUT INTO CUBES

1   2-POUND PACKAGE OF CHEESE FONDUE {FOUND IN SUPERMARKETS}

A fondue pot is a small investment that really pays off. Some cheese in the pot, a selection of breads and vegetables for dipping, and your guests can help themselves for the duration of the party.

Preheat the oven to 350°F. Toss the halved potatoes in the olive oil and sea salt. Spread in a single layer on a cookie sheet and bake for 30 minutes, or until tender. Cool for 15 minutes.

Toss the apples in the lemon juice. Arrange the potatoes, vegetables, apples, and bread cubes on a platter. Melt the cheese in a microwave oven on high for 3 to 5 minutes, or until completely melted, and transfer to fondue pot. Provide long fondue tongs for guests to use in dipping.

TIMESAVER: Buy precut vegetables in the produce section of the supermarket.

ELEGANT FRESH FRUIT SERVES 6

1   CUP FRESH LEMON JUICE

2   CUPS WATER

4   ASSORTED PEARS, QUARTERED

4   ASSORTED APPLES, QUARTERED

4   ASSORTED ORANGES, QUARTERED

2   POUNDS GREEN AND RED GRAPES, STEMMED

This is a beautiful way to decorate your special holiday gathering. Add your favorite seasonal fruit to the list below. You can also mix in shelled nuts.

In a large bowl, combine the lemon juice and water. Add the pears and apples. Let soak in the lemon water for 4 to 7 minutes. Drain and arrange as desired on a platter with the oranges and grapes.

TIMESAVER: Choose bite-sized fruit such as berries or set out a cutting board and a knife so guests can serve themselves.

SEARED SCALLOPS WITH EXOTIC SPICES _{SERVES 6}

1   *TEASPOON GROUND CUMIN*

1   *TEASPOON GROUND CORIANDER*

1   *TEASPOON GROUND NUTMEG*

1   *TEASPOON GROUND CLOVES*

1/4 *TEASPOON WHITE PEPPER*

12 *SEA SCALLOPS*

2   *TABLESPOONS CANOLA OIL*

Shrimp or fresh, firm-fleshed fish such as tuna adapts well to this preparation. For a special treat, sauté mango cubes in the pan along with the scallops.

In a small bowl, combine all the spices. Dust the scallops with the spice mixture. In a large sauté pan, heat the oil over high heat and sear the scallops for 2 minutes on each side, or until firm to the touch. Serve hot.

TIMESAVER: For large quantities, place the scallops on a well-oiled pan in a preheated 500°F oven and roast for 15 to 20 minutes, or until firm on the outside with tender centers.

BEEF AND MUSHROOM SKEWERS
WITH RED WINE SAUCE SERVES 6

2   TABLESPOONS CANOLA OIL

8   OUNCES FILET MIGNON, CUT INTO $^1/_2$-INCH CUBES

1   POUND SMALL CREMINI MUSHROOMS

$^1/_4$ CUP DRY RED WINE

    SALT AND FRESHLY GROUND PEPPER TO TASTE

2   TABLESPOONS MINCED FRESH FLAT-LEAF PARSLEY

Satisfy the meat-lovers in your group with these hearty hors d'oeuvres. The beef and mushrooms are cooked in a pan before threading onto skewers. For added flavor, use stripped rosemary branches to skewer the meat.

In a large sauté pan, heat the oil over high heat and sauté the filet and mushrooms for 10 to 15 minutes, or until meat is browned on the outside and slightly rare inside. Using a slotted spoon, transfer the meat and mushrooms to a bowl. Add the wine to the pan and cook for 2 to 3 minutes to reduce. Season with salt and pepper. Thread the beef and mushrooms on skewers and serve topped with red wine sauce and sprinkled with the parsley.

TIMESAVER: Skewer the mushrooms and beef raw. Place in a baking dish, add 1/4 cup of red wine, and bake in a 350°F oven for 20 to 30 minutes. Season with salt and pepper.

CHAPTER FIVE: COCKTAILS & HORS D'OEUVRES

SENSATIONAL SWEET NUTS MAKES 4 CUPS

1/2 CUP BALSAMIC VINEGAR

3 TABLESPOONS SUGAR

2 CUPS WALNUTS

2 CUPS PECANS

These irresistible snacks are addictive. Roast them ahead of time and keep them stored in an airtight container for up to five days.

Preheat the oven to 350°F. Line a jellyroll pan with parchment paper. In a large bowl, combine the balsamic vinegar and sugar. Add the nuts and toss to coat evenly. Spread the nuts evenly on the prepared pan and bake for 15 minutes, or until the mixture starts to bubble. Let cool completely before removing from the pan or serving.

TIMESAVER: Buy a selection of nuts from a nut shop or a gourmet market.

AT HOME WITH FRIENDS

NONALCOHOLIC GLÖGG SERVES 6 TO 8

1   BOTTLE {750 ML} BLACK CURRANT JUICE

     JUICE AND JULIENNED ZEST OF 1 ORANGE

1/2 CUP RAISINS

1   CINNAMON STICK

6   WHOLE CLOVES

2   CARDAMOM PODS, CRUSHED TO REVEAL SEEDS

1/4 CUP BLANCHED ALMONDS

Here's a nonalcoholic version of the traditional Swedish holiday drink. To make the traditional drink, replace the black currant juice with dry red wine and add 1/2 cup gin and 1/3 cup sugar.

In a large saucepan, stir the currant and orange juices and raisins together. Tie the orange zest, cinnamon, cloves, and cardamom in a cheesecloth square and add to the juice mixture. Bring to a simmer and cook for 10 minutes. Do not boil. Remove the spice bag and stir in the almonds.

TIMESAVER: Serve hot apple cider.

RESOURCES SOURCE GUIDE

PARTY SUPPLIES, CRAFT SUPPLIES, AND STATIONERY

AAHS
3223 Wilshire Boulevard
Santa Monica, CA 90403
310.829.1807
invitations, themed party supplies

KATE'S PAPERIE
561 Broadway
New York, NY 10012
212.941.9816
papers, invitations, craft supplies

MICHAEL'S ARTS & CRAFTS
972.409.7660
call for store locations
party supplies, craft supplies, holiday supplies

PAPER ACCESS
800.PAPER.01
catalog available
papers, stationery, envelopes

SOOLIP MARIE PAPIER
8574 Melrose Avenue
West Hollywood, CA 90069
310.360.0581
papers, stationery, cards, envelopes

SOOLIP PAPERIE
8646 Melrose Avenue
West Hollywood, CA 90069
310.360.0545
papers, stationery, cards, envelopes

STATS FLORAL SUPPLY
120 South Raymond Avenue
Pasadena, CA 91105
626.795.9308
party supplies, craft supplies, holiday supplies, silk flowers

FABRICS, NOTIONS, AND RIBBONS

B&J FABRICS
263 West 40th Street
New York, NY 10018
212.354.8150
fabrics

BELL'OCCHIO
8 Brady Street
San Francisco, CA 94103
415.864.4048
new and vintage ribbons

BRITEX FABRICS
146 Geary Street
San Francisco, CA 94108
415.392.2910
fabrics

F&S FABRICS
10629 West Pico Boulevard
Los Angeles, CA 90064
310.470.3398
fabrics, ribbons, trimmings

LINCOLN FABRICS
1600 Lincoln Boulevard
Venice, CA 90291
310.396.5724
fabrics, ribbons, trimmings, some vintage

HOUSEWARES

ABC CARPET & HOME
888 Broadway
New York, NY 10003
212.473.3000
home accessories, tableware, kitchenware, linens, candles

ANTHROPOLOGIE
800.309.2500
www.anthropologie.com
call for store locations or catalog
home accessories, tableware, kitchenware, linens, candles

BANANA REPUBLIC HOME
888.906.2800
www.bananarepublic.com
call for store locations or catalog
home accessories, tableware, linens, candles

BOUNTIFUL
1335 Abbot Kinney Boulevard
Venice, CA 90291
310.450.3620
home accessories, antique tableware, kitchenware

CALVIN KLEIN HOME
800.294.7978
call for store locations or catalog
home accessories, tableware

CONRAN SHOP
Michelin House
81 Fulham Road
London, England SW3
020.7589.7401
home accessories, tableware, kitchenware

COST PLUS WORLD MARKET
www.costplus.com
search for store locations online
tableware, kitchenware, linens, candles, outdoor entertaining, lighting, gourmet foods

CRATE & BARREL
800.451.8217
www.crateandbarrel.com
call for store locations or catalog
home accessories, tableware, kitchenware, linens, candles, outdoor entertaining

FRENCH GENERAL
35 Crosby Street
New York, NY 10013
212.343.7474
home accessories, tableware, linens

GLOBAL TABLE
107 Sullivan Street
New York, NY 10012
212.431.5839
home accessories, tableware, linens

HEAL AND SON LTD
196 Tottenham Court Road
London, England W1P 9LD
020.7636.1666
home accessories, tableware, kitchenware

HOMEWORK
1153 North Highland
Los Angeles, CA 90038
323.466.1153
home accessories, tableware, kitchenware

HOUSE
61.3.9347.9244
Australia
www.house-homewares.com.au
call for store locations
home accessories, tableware, kitchenware

IKEA
800.434.4532
www.ikea.com
call for store locations or catalog
home accessories, tableware, kitchenware, linens, lighting, outdoor entertaining

JOHN LEWIS PARTNERSHIP
278–306 Oxford Street
London, England W1
020.7629.7711
tableware

MAISON MIDI
150 South La Brea Avenue
Los Angeles, CA 90036
323.935.3154
tableware, linens

MEXICO ARTE
2242 West 4th Avenue
Vancouver, BC V6K 1N8
604.739.1767
tableware, linens

MING WO
2170 West 4th Avenue
Vancouver, BC V6K 1S9
604.737.2624
tableware, utensils

PEARL RIVER MART
277 Canal Street
New York, NY 10013
212.431.4770
www.pearlriver.com
Asian home accessories, tableware, kitchenware, lighting

POM POM
326 North La Brea Avenue
Los Angeles, CA 90036
323.934.2051
vintage home accessories, tableware, linens

POTTERY BARN
800.588.6250
www.potterybarn.com
call for store locations or catalog
*home accessories, tableware, linens,
candles, outdoor entertaining*

REJECT CHINA SHOP
183 Brompton Road
London, England SE3 1NU
020.7581.0739
tableware

RESTORATION HARDWARE
800.762.1005
www.restorationhardware.com
call for store locations or catalog
*home accessories, kitchenware,
candles, outdoor entertaining*

ROOM SERVICE
8115 3rd Street
Los Angeles, CA 90048
323.653.4242
home accessories, linens, candles

SHELTER
7920 Beverly Boulevard
Los Angeles, CA 90048
323.937.3222
*home accessories, tableware, linens,
candles*

SMITH & HAWKEN
800. 776.3336
www.smithandhawken.com
call for store locations or catalog
*home accessories, tableware, linens,
candles, plants, outdoor entertaining*

SOOLIP BUNGALOW
548 Norwich Drive
West Hollywood, CA 90048
310.360.1512
*home accessories, tableware, linens,
candles*

SUE FISHER KING
3067 Sacramento Street
San Francisco, CA 94115
415.922.7276
tableware, linens

SUPPLY AND DEMAND
567 Bridge Road
Richmond
Victoria, Australia 3121
61.3.9428.6912
www.supplyanddemand.com.au
*tableware, kitchen utensils,
accessories*

TARGET
800.800.8800
www.target.com
call for store locations
*tableware, kitchenware, linens,
candles, party supplies*

TROY
138 Greene Street
New York, NY 10012
212.941.4777
home accessories, candles

URBAN OUTFITTERS
800.282.2200
www.urbn.com
*home accessories, tableware,
lighting, candles*

WOLFMAN GOLD & GOOD CO.
117 Mercer Street
New York, NY 10012
212.431.1888
*home accessories, tableware, linens,
candles*

KITCHENWARE, BAKING
SUPPLIES, GOURMET FOODS

BALDUCCI'S
424 6th Avenue
New York, NY 10011
212.673.2600
gourmet foods

BROADWAY PANHANDLER
477 Broome Street
New York, NY 10013
212.966.3434
*tableware, kitchenware, linens,
baking supplies*

CHEF'S CATALOG
800.338.3232
www.chefscatalog.com
catalog and online shopping
*tableware, kitchenware,
baking supplies*

DEAN & DELUCA
800.999.0306
www.deananddeluca.com
call for store locations or catalog
*tableware, kitchenware,
gourmet foods*

JERRY'S HOME STORE
163–167 Fulham Road
London, England SW3 6SN
020.7335.2246
tableware, gourmet food

NY CAKE & BAKING
56 West 22nd Street
New York, NY 10010
212.675.2253
kitchenware, baking supplies

SUR LA TABLE
800.243.0852
www.surlatable.com
call for store locations or catalog
*tableware, kitchenware, linens,
baking supplies*

TRADER JOE'S
www.traderjoes.com
search for store locations online
*discount gourmet groceries,
fresh flowers*

WILLIAMS SONOMA
800.541.2233
www.williams-sonoma.com
*tableware, kitchenware, linens,
candles, outdoor entertaining,
gourmet foods*

FLOWERS/GARDENING

HORTUS
284 E. Orange Grove Boulevard
Pasadena, CA 91104
626.792.8255
plants, flowers, gifts

MELLANO & COMPANY
766 Wall Street
Los Angeles, CA 90014
213.622.0796
fresh cut flowers and foliage

RENTALS

ABSOLUTE PARTY RENTAL
836 Ritchie Highway, Suite 19
Severna Park, MD 21146
410.544.7474

CLASSIC PARTY RENTALS
8476 Stellar Drive
Culver City, CA 90232
310.202.0011

INDEX

TABLE OF EQUIVALENTS

LIQUID/DRY MEASURES

U.S.	METRIC
1/4 TEASPOON	1.25 MILLILITERS
1/2 TEASPOON	2.5 MILLILITERS
1 TEASPOON	5 MILLILITERS
1 TABLESPOON (3 teaspoons)	15 MILLILITERS
1 FLUID OUNCE (2 tablespoons)	30 MILLILITERS
1/4 CUP	60 MILLILITERS
1/3 CUP	80 MILLILITERS
1/2 CUP	120 MILLILITERS
1 CUP	240 MILLILITERS
1 PINT (2 cups)	480 MILLILITERS
1 QUART (4 cups, 32 ounces)	960 MILLILITERS
1 GALLON (4 QUARTS)	3.84 LITERS
1 OUNCE (by weight)	28 GRAMS
1 POUND	454 GRAMS
2.2 POUNDS	1 KILOGRAM

LENGTH

U.S.	METRIC
1/8 INCH	3 MILLIMETERS
1/4 INCH	6 MILLIMETERS
1/2 INCH	12 MILLIMETERS
1 INCH	2.5 CENTIMETERS

OVEN TEMPERATURE

FAHRENHEIT	CELSIUS	GAS
250	120	1/2
275	140	1
300	150	2
325	160	3
350	180	4
375	190	5
400	200	6
425	220	7
450	230	8
475	240	9
500	260	10